Dearest Clare,

My baby, I hope this brings back memories of your time in Africa but also lets you think and plan for the amazing memories we will have in Africa. There are undoubtedly some of the most beautiful sunsets (☺) and I can't wait to share them with you!!

All my love
Bruce
xxx

AFRICA

continent of contrasts

AFRICA
continent of contrasts

PHILIP BRIGGS

photography by
MARTIN HARVEY & ARIADNE VAN ZANDBERGEN

C O N T

E N T S

FRONT COVER. African
elephant (*Loxodonta africana*)
in silhouette against the sunset
in Etosha National Park,
Namibia.

PAGE 1. A Swahili girl relaxes
against a carved Zanzibari door
in the Tanzanian backwater
of Bagamoyo.

PAGES 2–3. The stone town
of Zanzibar is the largest
enclave of traditional Swahili
architecture in existence.

PAGES 4–5. Burchell's Zebra
walk through a dry-season dust
storm in Namibia's Etosha Pan.

THIS PAGE. Poling a pirogue
along the Niger River near
Timbuktu.

OVERLEAF. The weekly
market at Sanga on Mali's
Bandiagara Escarpment.

First published in 2005 by New Holland Publishers (UK) Ltd
London • Cape Town • Sydney • Auckland

2 4 6 8 10 9 7 5 3 1

www.newhollandpublishers.com

Garfield House, 86–88 Edgware Road, London W2 2EA, UK
80 McKenzie Street, Cape Town 8001, South Africa
14 Aquatic Drive, Frenchs Forest, NSW 2086, Australia
218 Lake Road, Northcote, Auckland, New Zealand

ISBN 1 84537 222 0

Publishing manager: Pippa Parker
Managing editor: Lynda Harvey
Project manager: Francesca Butler
Editor: Emily Bowles
Designer: Janice Evans
Proofreader: Tessa Kennedy
Cartographer: David du Plessis

Publisher's Note: The author and publishers have made every effort to
ensure that the information contained in this book was correct at the time
of going to press, and they accept no responsibility for any loss, injury or
inconvenience sustained by any person through using this book.

Reproduction by: Hirt & Carter
Printed and bound by: Tien Wah Press (Pte) Ltd

ACKNOWLEDGEMENTS

Philip Briggs and Ariadne Van Zandbergen would like to thank Wilderness Safaris and Fuji Films for their assistance in researching this book.

Martin Harvey would like to thank Dr Stuart Williams and the staff of the Ethiopian Wolf Conservation Project, the staff of Chumbe Island Coral Park, Aletta Jordaan of Cape Nature Conservation, Marlice van der Merwe of Harnas Wildlife Foundation, Lesedi Cultural Village, Jeff Gaisford and staff of KZN Wildlife, Beverly Pervan and Chris Mercer of the Kalahari Raptor Centre, Rita Bachmann and staff of Unusual Destinations, Treehaven Waterfowl Trust, Mrs M. Kapere and staff of the Ministry of Environment and Tourism, Namibia, the Reillys of Big Game Parks, Swaziland, Arno Naude of Reptile Wrangler, Andrea Turkalo of the Wildlife Conservation Society, Liz Pearson and Amos Courage of The John Aspinall Foundation, Sheila and David Siddle of Chimfunshi, Jean Wickings of CIRMF Gabon, Annette Lanjouw of the African Wildlife Foundation, Hayat Aharrar of the South African Embassy in Morocco, Michele Depraz of WWF International, Apenheul Primate Park in the Netherlands as well as all the many people who modelled and allowed him to photograph them. His sincere appreciation goes to Jessica White and Jonathan and Thalita Harvey who all contributed help and support.

INTRODUCTION

The notion of Africa as a single unified entity is an exotic one. Indeed, the very name Africa is Roman in origin, possibly derived from the Greek 'Aphrike' (meaning 'not cold'), more likely a reference to a Berber tribe called the Afri, and was first applied to a province of present-day Tunisia after the Punic Wars. At that time, the Greek term 'Aethiopia' – Land of Burnt-skinned People – was more normally used to refer to sub-Saharan Africa, a region whose full southerly extent remained a matter of conjecture prior to 1488, when the Portuguese navigator Bartolomeu Dias rounded the Cape of Good Hope to open a trade route between the Atlantic and Indian oceans.

In an era dominated by terrestrial and aerial modes of transport, it is easy to forget that the great oceanic expanses once formed less of an obstacle to travel than the land-masses they divided. When Dias first rounded the Cape, for instance, the Indian Ocean supported a centuries-old maritime trade linking the east coast of Africa to Arabia and Asia, while the Atlantic was emerging as a trade passage between West Africa, Europe and the Americas. By contrast, much of the African interior – its great rivers, lakes, waterfalls and mountains – would go undocumented by outsiders for another 350 years. In fact, many European geographers greeted initial mid-nineteenth-century reports of snow-capped peaks and vast inland seas set in the equatorial heart of the so-called Dark Continent with rank scepticism.

As for the name Africa, though outsiders had used it for centuries prior to the Victorian Era, it would have been unfamiliar to the majority of the continent's inhabit-ants at that time. In 1850, the East African Maasai or Baganda would have been wholly ignorant of the existence of the Sotho or Tswana of southern Africa, who in turn knew nothing of West Africa's Dogon or Pygmies – and if a few individuals among these diverse sub-Saharan people were familiar with the ancient civilizations of North Africa, then it would have been through the external medium of missionaries, explorers or traders. At that time, it was not merely the name Africa, but the very concept of Africa – as one place, as one continent – that would have meant nothing to most of the people who lived there.

Colonialism followed the Victorian exploration of the African interior so closely that the two processes form a historical blur, with colonialism often perceived to be the inevitable consequence of exploration. Yet the reality is more complex. Certainly, acquisitiveness played a large role in the so-called 'Scramble for Africa'. However, so did

RIGHT: A Cape Gannet coming in to land at the breeding colony off the west coast of southern Africa.
OVERLEAF: Young Maasai dancers leap into the air from a standing position, in order to demonstrate their strength and agility.

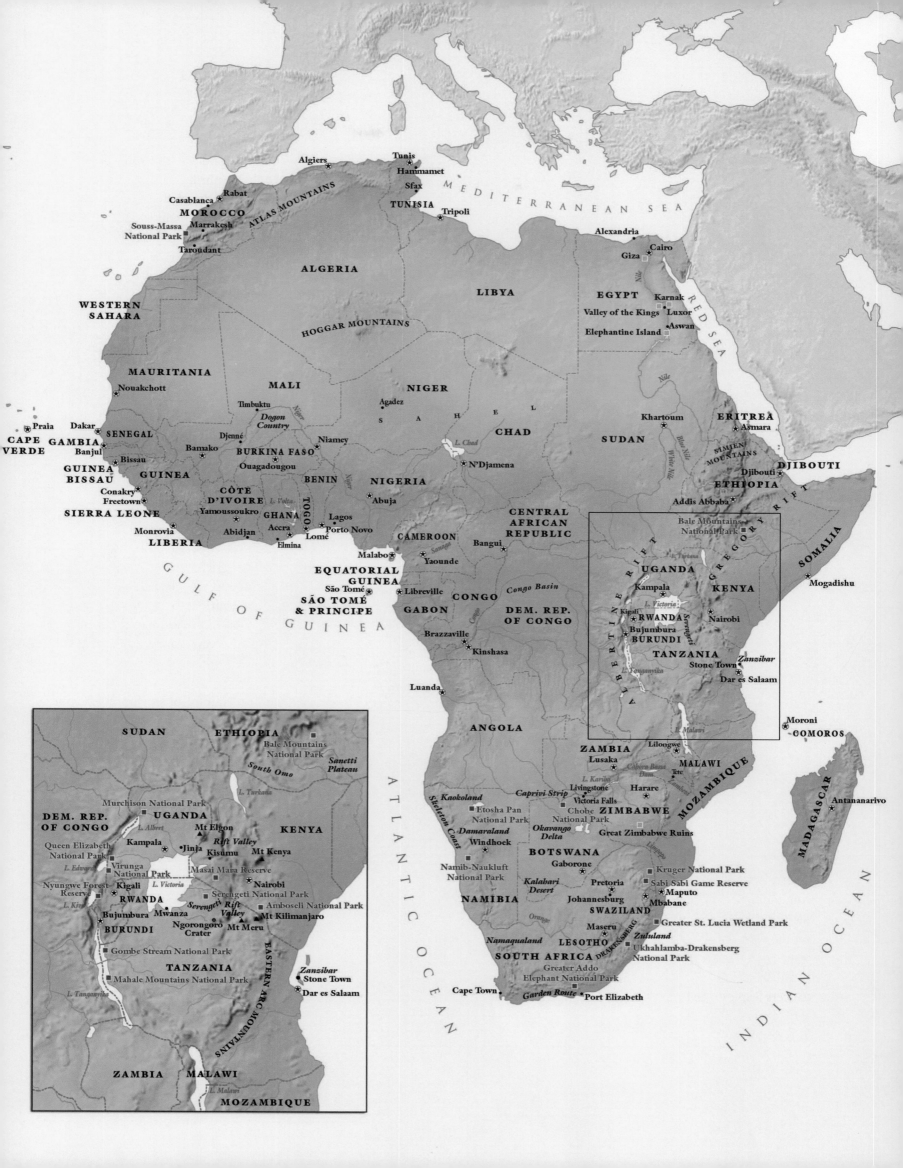

liberal idealism: most specifically the desire to establish legitimate commerce in place of the traffic in human lives that had resulted in the export of perhaps 20 million African captives to the Americas and Indian Ocean islands between the sixteenth and late nineteenth centuries. If the notion of Africa as a single entity is exotic, then so too are the lines that divide its constituent countries. These arbitrary constructs were delineated over the conference tables of Victorian Europe, with borders that cut willy-nilly across ethnic lines, while often forcing tribes together who formerly shared nothing other than a history of mutual animosity.

Outsiders still tend to think of Africa as one place. Tourists talk of going to Africa rather than to the specific country they are visiting, journalists and bar-room theorists generalize glibly about African politics as if no international border divided the Cape from Cairo, and Afrophobics latch onto any isolated tragedy – a famine in Ethiopia, an Ebola outbreak in the Congo, a war in Liberia – as further evidence that the continent's heart remains inherently dark, dangerous and disorderly. This monolithic vision of Africa is as conceptually absurd as talking about a monolithic Europe that includes the likes of Portugal, Germany, Ireland, Sweden and Croatia. Indeed, it is probably more absurd, since it is close to impossible to make any meaningful generalization about a continent whose cultural, ethnic and geographic diversity embraces nations as diverse as Libya and Lesotho, Mali and Malawi, Egypt and Mozambique, or Ethiopia and Mauritania. Many single African countries – Tanzania, for instance, or South Africa – contain a diversity of landscapes and cultures sufficient to populate an entire continent!

Of course, there is also much that links the scattered corners of the world's second-largest continent, much that genuinely does come across as archetypically and almost universally African. A busy local market in Ghana is not so different in feel to a busy local market in Uganda or Mozambique. The few remaining elephants that roam the West African savanna might easily have been transplanted there from Tanzania or Zambia. The gaudily painted *matatus* that hurtle recklessly around Nairobi have a clear counterpart in the lunatic taxis that twitch and lurch with suicidal glee through downtown Cairo. The confiding bulbuls that chatter cheerfully in the gardens of suburban Johannesburg are practically indistinguishable from those that flap above the Roman ruins in Libya and Tunisia. And at the risk of delving into the realm of cliché, the people of Africa, despite their immense cultural diversity, do seem to possess several common traits – a marked religious and social conservatism by comparison with their European neighbours, a somewhat philosophical attitude towards the future, and a *joie de vivre* that shines through in the most humble, even deprived, of living conditions.

This book is essentially a visual celebration of Africa's diversity – its incomparable wealth of traditional cultures, its underrated historical and archaeological treasures, its peerless herds of wildlife, and its often larger-than-life scenery. As such, the photography tends to dwell on the natural and the traditional rather than the artificial or the modern. True enough, great cities such as Johannesburg, Nairobi and Lagos are integral to contemporary Africa, and their mood of cosmopolitan urbanity almost certainly forms a more realistic pointer to the continent's future than do the last few remaining hunter-gatherers in the Kalahari, or the Great Pyramids of Giza, or the migrating wildebeest of the Serengeti, or the retracting snow that caps Kilimanjaro. But then the most obvious single generalization that can be made about Africa since it became Africa, little more than a century ago, is that it has changed almost beyond recognition, with every passing year bringing fresh losses in biodiversity, further destruction of irreplaceable habitats, and greater cultural homogeneity. Even so, Africa is still a continent of astonishing natural and cultural abundance and variety, and this book is dedicated to the preservation of the wealth that remains.

OPPOSITE: A newborn yellow baboon, like a human infant, is dependent on the continuous care of an adult.

15

NORTH AFRICA

The saline water of the Mediterranean forms a far less formidable barrier than the sandy Sahara desert. It should come as no surprise, then, that the relatively small tract of arable African soil sandwiched between these two great geographical landmarks shares little in terms of history or culture or ecology with the far greater portion of Africa that stretches south from the Sahel (the band of dry savanna forming the southern boundary of the Sahara) to the Cape. Indeed, viewed from a continental perspective, North Africa is something of an anomaly: culturally, it feels more like a western extension of Arabia than a northern extension of the sub-Saharan region, while its historical links to Mediterranean Europe, with which it has engaged in periodic wars since Roman times, seem far stronger than those binding it to the rest of Africa.

And yet, despite being situated at the cultural and historical junction of three continents, North Africa does possess a distinctive character all its own. Fundamentally Islamic, the region comes across as somewhat more outward looking and tolerant than its Arabian counterparts: alcoholic drinks, for instance, are brewed and sold legally in most parts of North Africa, while several countries support significant non-Islamic religious minorities, most notably Egypt with its six million Christian Copts. Ethnically, North Africa defies easy categorization. Over the millennia, its indigenous blend of Caucasian and Semitic roots has been regularly infused with fresh blood from south of the Sahara, north of the Mediterranean, and east of the Gulf of Suez.

The inhospitable nature of the Sahara notwithstanding, North Africa has not evolved in absolute isolation from the rest of the continent. Almost certainly, it was through a limited early desert trade that agriculture, domestic livestock and crafts such as iron smelting first

OPPOSITE: Islamic women, adorned in traditional *chadors* or *nikabs* (cloaks), walk past a colourful abstract mural depicting Muslim women in Taroudant, Morocco.

BELOW: Intricate stuccowork and wood carvings embellish the courtyard of the sixteenth-century theological school of Ali ben Youssef in Marrakech.

took root in the Sahel before progressing gradually southward to the Cape. The growth in the trans-Sahara trade after AD 500 encouraged the spread of Islam into West Africa and the foundation of the great Muslim cities of the Sahel, most famously Timbuktu and Djenné. And, while the Islam faith reached the eastern shores of Africa via trade with the Arabian gulf, it was indirect contact with the Egyptian Copts that led to the adoption of Christianity as the state religion of Ethiopia in the fourth century. Furthermore, the wealth of gold carried across the Sahara from West Africa to the Mediterranean was one of the main inspirations for the fifteenth-century Portuguese exploration of the Atlantic coastline, leading to the first direct contact between Europe and sub-Saharan Africa.

North Africa's historical centrepiece is, of course, Egypt and the Nile Valley. The rich antiquities here span almost 4 000 years of Pharaonic rule. Among them, the iconic pyramids at Giza, the brooding tombs carved into the Valley of the Kings, and the decorously magnificent Karnak Temple stand as the world's oldest tourist attractions, having bedazzled European sightseers in Roman times much as they do today. And while the East African Rift Valley is widely believed to be a pivotal site in the history of human evolution, North Africa must be regarded as the cradle of learning and civilization. Egypt, in particular, doesn't merely stand at the junction of three continents, but also forms the very cornerstone of modern civilization.

BELOW: The palm tree thrives in the desert sands.
BELOW CENTRE: A statue of Tuthmosis III, circa 1450, in Luxor Museum.
BOTTOM: Smoking a *sheesha* – a traditional bubble pipe – is a popular pastime in Egypt.

19

Metropolis of the world

CAIRO AND THE GIZA PYRAMIDS

The largest and most chaotic city anywhere in Africa or the Middle East, Cairo straddles the Nile 150 kilometre southeast of its mouth near Alexandria. It lies just 20 kilometres north of the ruined city of Memphis, which was founded more than 5 000 years ago, prior to the Pharaonic period, as the world's first imperial capital. One medieval scribe lauded Cairo as 'the metropolis of the world, the garden of the universe, the meeting place of nations [and] a human ant heap', a description that still feels apt some 600 years later, as the great city's population soars ever closer to the 20-million mark.

Modern Cairo, or more accurately Al-Qahira, is often said to have been founded in AD 969, when the Fatamid General Gawhar decided to build an imperial capital on the west bank of the Nile. He named it in honour of the planet Mars (Al Qahir means 'the victorious' in Arabic), which was in the ascendant at the time. In truth, however, Cairo is much older than this story would suggest: the modern suburb of Heliopolis stands on the site of a pre-Christian Roman city known at that time as Babylon. Similarly, the old Coptic quarter of present-day Cairo probably dates to the third century AD and the Islamic quarter known as al-Fustat was founded in AD 642 by Khalif Omar, second of the four successors to the Prophet Mohammed.

No settlement of note graced the site of Cairo in Pharaonic times, but the city's eastern suburbs do verge on what is justifiably the most celebrated of all ancient Egyptian monuments, and the only one of the Seven Wonders of the Ancient World to have survived to the present day, namely the Pyramids of Giza. Built primarily as tombs by the Fourth Dynasty Pharaohs Khufu, Khafre and Menkaure, who ruled between 2551 and 2472 BC, the main trio of pyramids at Giza are the bulkiest constructions of their sort in the world. The method by which they were constructed remains the subject of some architectural – and mystical – conjecture.

The largest pyramid at Giza (a geometric colossus that consists of roughly 2,3 million limestone blocks, weighing an average of 2,5 tons apiece) was built by Khufu (also known as Cheops) and rises from a 53 000-square-metre base to a height of 146 metres. No less iconic than Khufu's Pyramid is the immense limestone statue whose mysterious feline gaze leads away from Giza towards the nearby banks of the Nile. Measuring 57 metres in length and 20 metres in height, the Great Sphinx – whose half-human, half-lion appearance inspired the local Arabic name Abu Hel or 'the Father of Terror' – was carved into a natural limestone spur some 4 500 years ago, and has spent much of the subsequent period partially or fully buried under the desert sands.

OPPOSITE: The mosque of Amr ibn al-As, constructed circa 650 BC, was the first mosque built in Cairo and remains one of the oldest in the world. BELOW AND OVERLEAF: The celebrated camel market at Birqash, on the northern outskirts of Cairo.

BELOW: The pyramids at Giza. Khafre (in the background) is the only one that retains some of its original limestone cover.
OPPOSITE ABOVE: The Sphinx has gazed out towards the Nile for longer than four millenia.
OPPOSITE BELOW LEFT: The golden mask of Tutankhamen.
OPPOSITE BELOW RIGHT: The tomb of Khenu at Saqqara, with the deceased and his son portrayed on a pillar.
OVERLEAF: The step pyramid built by the Pharaoh Djoser in the twenty-sixth century BC dominates the necropolis of Saqqara.

The monuments at Giza are the best known of almost 100 pyramids that rise from the otherwise empty Saharan sands running westward from the site of ancient Memphis and the modern-day sprawl of Cairo. Among the most impressive and oldest of these is the 58-metre-high Step Pyramid built for the Third Dynasty Pharaoh Djoser in around 2620 BC. It is the centrepiece of a sprawling 15-hectare necropolis at Saqqara, about 20 kilometres south of Giza, and is studded with ornately sculpted and painted subterranean tombs.

And yet despite its proximity to the world's most celebrated antiquities, Cairo today comes across as an emphatically modern city, one whose caffeine-soaked mood of insomnia and strikingly varied architecture place it at the very juncture of Arabia, Europe and Africa. There is the modern city centre, where perpetual horn-bashing traffic jams are hemmed in by smoke-grey art deco monoliths, and of course the Nile itself. This life-sustaining natural corridor is overlooked by unquestionably the finest museum anywhere on the continent, home – among other things – to the superb collection of antiquities unearthed in the tomb of Tutankhamen.

However, the older eastern quarters that are collectively referred to as Islamic Cairo are the most fascinating part of the city. They are a bustling mosaic of ancient mosques, chaotic markets, faded caravanserais and timeworn coffee shops. The imposing Al-Qala or Citadel dominates the scene – an immense hilltop fortress built by Sultan Saladin in 1176 and expanded during the mid-nineteenth century reign of Mohammed Ali. Flanked by the mighty pyramids and bisected by the wide waters of the Nile, this is quite simply – and with all due respect to Capetonians – the most compelling, captivating and confusing of all African cities.

River of the pharaohs

THE NILE VALLEY

The Nile is an inseparable part of the history and culture of Egypt. Without the Nile, and the water and silt it carries northward from the tropics, there would have been no opportunity for agriculture to take root in Egypt. Nor would this barley- and wheat-growing society have developed into the world's first and most historically enduring centralized civilization. Pharaonic Egypt first took shape in around 4000 BC and thrived for more than three millennia. It fell into terminal decline during an extended period of Hellenic influence that began with the conquest of Egypt by Alexander the Great in 332 BC, and ended with the suicide of Cleopatra VII some 300 years later.

The archaeological treasures of the Nile Valley are unparalleled, and they span the entire period from 4000 BC to around AD 600. Relics of the Old Kingdom, such as the Giza Pyramids and Great Sphinx, are centred in the north of Egypt, close to the ancient capital of Memphis and its modern-day counterpart Cairo. In around 1550 BC, however, political power shifted southward to Weset (now known as Luxor after the Arabic phrase Al-Uqsur – 'The Castles' – and also sometimes referred to by its Greek name, Thebes). This formerly obscure riverside village rose to become the capital of the New Kingdom as well as the site of two of the most elaborate temples ever constructed in ancient times.

Today, Luxor and its environs warrant several days' exploration. Luxor Temple dominates the central riverfront. It is a vast colonnaded complex founded by Amenophis III in about 1400 BC, when it was dedicated to the deities Amun, Mut and Khonso. A century later, Rameses II expanded Luxor and immense statues of him still dominate the high entrance. Vaster and more impressive still is the leviathan Karnak Temple, which extends over 50 hectares on the northern edge of the town centre. Dominated by the giddying Hypostyle Hall – with its immense pillars that reach towards the sky like a concrete forest – Karnak is also notable for several superb statues of various pharaohs as well as obelisks of solid pink granite standing up to 23 metres tall.

The Theban Necropolis, which runs inland of the west bank of the Nile opposite Luxor, is where the Pharaohs of the New Kingdom were buried, as were most other members of the royal family and important administrators and officials. Here you'll find the Valley of the Kings, site of some 60 Pharaonic tombs. Their elaborately decorated walls look almost as breathtakingly vibrant today as they must have when they were first painted over 3 000 years ago. The most famous figure interred here is Tutankhamen, whose tomb lay undisturbed by grave robbers prior to being discovered by the archaeologist Howard Carter in November 1922. Other tombs in the valley include several of the Rameses as well as the only female Pharaoh of the New Kingdom, Hatshepsut.

OPPOSITE: The Ramesseum, built by the all-conquering Pharaoh Rameses II in the thirteenth century BC, is one of the most impressive of the ancient Theban temples on the west bank of the Nile, facing Luxor.
BELOW: A bas-relief and hieroglyphics engraved into the wall of the temple of Medinet Habu near Luxor.
OVERLEAF: The modern village of Gurnat Murai has a rich historical setting at the base of the arid mountains housing the legendary Valley of the Kings.

OPPOSITE: Engraved more than 3 000 years ago, the magnificent bas-reliefs on the colonnades in the second court of the temple of Medinet Habu remain remarkably well preserved.

LEFT: A 1300 BC painting of Rameses I and Horus, the falcon-like God of the Sky, in the burial chamber of Rameses I in the Valley of the Kings.

RIGHT: This colossal head at the Ramesseum, part of a decapitated statue, is one of several monuments to the temple's constructor, Rameses II.

BELOW: The Osiris pillars in the courtyard of the temple of Rameses III in Karnak.

The angular temple built by Hatshepsut into a nearby granite cliff is one of the most modern-looking Pharaonic constructions, and contains a thought-provoking series of murals. They depict a naval expedition to a land called Punt – probably in modern-day Somalia or Eritrea – that returned with a wealth of animal pelts, scented wood and spices. Also of note are the classical colonnaded temples built on the west bank by Rameses II and Rameses III, and the colourfully decorated tombs that dot the Valley of the Queens and the so-called Worker's Village – many equally as fascinating and well preserved as their counterparts in the Valley of the Kings.

The bustling market town of Aswan is situated above an unnavigable cataract now submerged by the Aswan Dam. The ancients knew the town as Syrene ('market'), in reference to its importance – or rather the importance of the facing Elephantine Island – as a centre of trade with the people of Nubia to the south. Several important tombs and temples lie in the vicinity of Aswan and Elephantine, and the city also serves as the springboard for visiting Abu Simbel, which is arguably the most imposing of all the New Kingdom temples. Distinguished by the gargantuan statues of Rameses II and his wife Nefertari that line the entrance to its two intricately carved temples, Abu Simbel is remarkable for two reasons. Firstly, it went unseen for millennia prior to being rediscovered by a Swiss explorer in the early nineteenth century, and secondly it was relocated, block-by-block, to its present site in the late 1960s, to prevent it from being submerged by the Aswan Dam.

BELOW: The ruined city of Yebu lies on Elephantine Island in the Nile, opposite the modern port of Aswan.
OPPOSITE: Consisting of a single carved block of granite, a 25-metre-high obelisk towers above a colossal statue of Rameses II in the Luxor Temple.
OVERLEAF: The Sharia as-Souq, the most important market in Aswan, is busiest during the cool of the evening.

The Nile

The world's longest river, the Nile flows for 6 650 kilometres from its most remote headwater to its Mediterranean delta, and drains more than 10 per cent of Africa's surface area en route. It is the lifeblood of Egyptian agriculture, carrying water and silt from the fertile tropics into areas that receive less than 25 millimetres of rain annually. Its flood plain nurtured the first agricultural societies as well as the most enduring of all human civilizations. The antiquity of the name Nile, literally 'river valley', is reflected in the ancient Greek Nelios, the Semetic Nahal and the Latin Nilus.

The Nile's two major sources, the White and Blue Nile, flow out of Uganda's Lake Victoria and Ethiopia's Lake Tana respectively, to merge at the Sudanese capital of Khartoum. The eighteenth-century Scots explorer James Bruce is often credited with the discovery of the Blue Nile's source, even though it had been visited by Portuguese explorers 200 years earlier, and was also known to the ancients. (The Old Testament asserts that the Nile 'compasseth the whole land of Ethiopia'. This was a reference to its arcing course along the southern boundary of the Axumite Empire, i.e. historical Ethiopia.)

By contrast, the source of the White Nile was, for centuries, one of the world's great, unsolved mysteries. The Emperor Nero once sent an expedition to search for it, but his men were forced to turn back at the Sudd, a 5,5 million-hectare swamp in southern Sudan. In 1862, Speke identified Lake Victoria as the source of the White Nile, but it was only in 1937 that Waldecker located its most remote headwater, the source of the Kagera River, in Burundi.

Over the past 50 years, several hydroelectric dams have been built along the Nile, notably the Aswan Dam in Egypt and the Owen Falls Dam in Uganda. The waterway's importance to the survival of several wetland mammals and birds would be difficult to overstate. The Sudd alone supports more than half the global populations of Nile lechwe and Shoebills, together with 1,7 million Glossy Ibises, 370 000 Marabou Storks, 350 000 Open-billed Storks, 175 000 Cattle Egrets, and 150 000 Spur-winged Geese.

ABOVE: The Nile and its associated waterways are home to the papyrus-dwelling Shoebill.
BELOW: Uganda's Murchison Falls.
OPPOSITE ABOVE: Feluccas on the Nile at Aswan and (BELOW) sunset over the Victoria Nile in Uganda.

Land of the setting sun

THE MAGHREB

An ancient Arabic term meaning 'land of the setting sun', the name Maghreb has long been used to refer to the most westerly part of the established Islamic world. This region is traditionally regarded as encompassing Morocco (also known as al-Maghreb al-Aqsa i.e. 'the farthest Maghreb') along with Algeria and Tunisia to its east. In more recent times, the extent of al-Maghreb al-Kabir – 'The Greater Maghreb' – has been expanded through formal political alliances to include Mauritania and Libya, both of which share strong historical and cultural links with the other Maghreb states.

The oldest inhabitants of the Maghreb are the Berbers, a non-Semitic Caucasoid people whose name derives from an ancient Greek word applied to all non-Greek speakers. Also known as the Imazighen, the Berber people traditionally speak a variety of mutually intelligible dialects of Amazigh. Although in the cities Arabic and French have usurped the language, it is still spoken by some 10 million inhabitants of Algeria, Morocco and Tunisia, mostly within rural communities. Berber blood and culture has received numerous infusions over the millennia – from across the Mediterranean, from across the Red Sea and from across the Sahara – with the result that many individuals are somewhat Iberian in appearance, while others look West African. Indeed, the region as a whole, despite its strong Islamic following, can sometimes come across as being closer in mood to Mediterranean Europe than any other part of Africa or Arabia.

The warlike and independent Berbers managed to resist attempts at Spanish and French colonization until 1933. Though ethnically cohesive, they accommodate a blend of religions and cultures, having alternately resisted and accepted new beliefs and political regimes over the past two millennia. They are predominantly Islamic, though several Christian and a smaller number of Jewish communities still persist, particularly in Tunisia and Morocco. Some Berbers lead a nomadic lifestyle, most famously perhaps the Tuareg, the blue-robed cameleers who have controlled the trans-Sahara caravan trade practically since its inception. Others are settled pastoralists and many farm a mixture of small livestock, olives, almonds and various grains.

The Atlas Mountains were the main centre of Berber resistance to colonization. This imposing spine-like range forms the natural barrier between the coastal belt of Morocco and Algeria and the wastes of the Saharan interior. The tallest mountain range in North Africa, the High Atlas of Morocco boasts more than a dozen peaks that top the

PREVIOUS PAGE: Curiously modern in appearance, the Deir Al Bahari was constructed by the female Pharaoh Hatshepsut below the rocky Theban Hills in the fifteenth century BC. OPPOSITE: A fortified Berber kasbah in the Dades Valley below the Atlas Mountains. ABOVE LEFT: A decorated enclave in the Ait Benhaddou kasbah near Ourzazate. ABOVE RIGHT: Migratory White Storks nest on the minaret of a mosque in the Dades Valley, Morocco.

43

Islam

The Islamic faith was founded by the Prophet Mohammed, who was born in AD 570, orphaned eight years later, and worked the trade caravans out of Mecca prior to marrying his twice-widowed employer Khadija at the age of 25. Some 15 years later, Mohammed was visited by the Archangel Gabriel and received the first of the lessons that would form the basis of the Five Pillars of Islam, namely faith, prayer, almsgiving, fasting and pilgrimage.

Mohammed's preaching angered the ruling classes in Mecca, so in AD 622 – following the death of his wife and uncle – he fled to an oasis called Medina, where he received wide support until his death in AD 632. Remarkably, within just 20 years of this, Islam was entrenched as the main religion of Arabia, and the hadj – the prophet's pilgrimage to Medina – had been adopted as the beginning of the Arabic calendar.

Oddly enough, the first part of Africa to be settled by Mohammed's followers was Christian Ethiopia. In AD 615, the Axumite King allowed some Islamic exiles – the prophet's wife Khadija temporarily among them – to settle at Negash, the founding place of eastern Ethiopia's extant Muslim community. By the twelfth century, Islam had taken root in several Swahili coastal ports, from Mogadishu to Mozambique, as a result of maritime trade. But Islam's strongest sphere of African influence has always been north of the Sahara, where, following the Arab conquests of the late seventh century, it had usurped Christianity by AD 800, and then spread across the Sahel along the caravan routes.

Many Westerners expect Islamic Africa to be hostile to Christian visitors. But this is seldom the case, provided that local sensibilities are accorded due respect. There are many parts of Africa – from Ethiopia to Ghana, from Cairo to Cape Town, from Dar es Salaam to Kampala – where long-standing Christian and Islamic communities live and work alongside each other, and have done so for decades, in a broadly amicable atmosphere. Indeed, in this respect Africans are exemplary in their attitude of religious tolerance.

ABOVE: It is conventional for Muslims and other visitors to take off their shoes before entering a mosque.
BELOW: An Islamic woman in a traditional cloak.
OPPOSITE: Morocco's Djemaa el-Fna marketplace and Koutoubia Mosque.

4 000-metre mark. This range stands in dramatic contrast to the sandy, sun-drenched plains from which it rises, with its middle slopes draped in cedar, conifer and other evergreen forests, and its upper reaches regularly buried under snow during winter. Still very rustic, the Atlas Mountains remain a stronghold for traditional Berber sheep- and goat-herding cultures to this day.

In the south of Tunisia, the local Berber tribes are known for their striking traditional architecture. Around Matmata, for instance, they practise a troglodyte lifestyle, living in artificial caves carved into the walls of deep circular subterranean pits. Further south, fortified villages such as Chenini and Douiret are even more ruggedly memorable, set as they are on remote craggy hilltops where the stone and wood dwellings, some still inhabited, have been expanded from natural caves and cliffs. The reasoning behind this unique but satisfyingly organic architectural style remains a matter of conjecture: defensibility must be a factor, along with the relative coolness of the naturally ventilated cave dwellings, even in the heat of the midday summer sun.

PREVIOUS PAGE: The *ksar* at the south Tunisian village of Ouled Soltane is essentially a fortified granary, whose *ghorfas*, or cells, were used for the storage of grain.
BELOW: The fortified hill village of Douiret in southern Tunisia.

LEFT: Henna powder, mixed with lemon juice, cloves and rosewater to give its characteristic rusty colour, is used to decorate women's hands and feet.

BELOW LEFT: A Berber nomad takes a break from loading her donkey in the Atlas Mountains.

BELOW RIGHT: A young woman weaves a traditional carpet in a typical rural village in Morocco.

OVERLEAF: A Berber shepherd tends his livestock in the High Atlas region of Oukaimeden, Morocco.

Markets

A somewhat obsolete institution in most Western societies, the market lies at the core of village and small-town economies throughout Africa. It is also a pivotal social event, offering an opportunity for friends, relatives and other acquaintances living in outlying communities to stock up, dress up and catch up on all the latest gossip and news.

In most parts of Africa, the main market in any given town or village is held weekly, allowing local traders to set up stall in several different communities over the course of seven days. In Ethiopia's South Omo region, for instance, the Hamer village of Arbore holds its main market on Saturday, while Weita, 50 kilometres to the north, hosts a big market on Sunday, and Turmi to the south takes its turn on Monday. Experienced African travellers usually plan their itineraries in such areas around market days, since they offer the best opportunity to interact with local cultures, though such planning is trickier in parts of West Africa where market days rotate on four-, five- or six-day cycles.

Africa offers several highlights to aficionados of traditional markets. For overall impact, the Monday market below Mali's Djenné Mosque is hard to beat, while Kumasi's Kejetia market and Addis Ababa's sprawling Mercato, which operate daily, could plausibly be the largest markets in sub-Saharan Africa. The vast fetish market outside the Togolese capital of Lomé is probably the most macabre event of its type on the continent.

In keeping with Islamic customs elsewhere, markets to the north of the Sahara, often referred to as bazaars, tend to be integrated into the *medina* or town centre, with different alleys reserved for different types of trade since mediaeval times. Sadly, tourism has subverted many of the region's best known markets, particularly around coastal resorts, where the medina tends to be swamped with ingratiating stall-owners selling identical souvenirs. By contrast, the region's city markets – the likes of Sfax, Tunis and even Cairo – remain absorbing and infinitely exotic monuments to our common consumerism.

ABOVE: A Peul trader at Djenné market.
BELOW: Hair softener on sale at a market in Bahir Dar, northern Ethiopia.
OPPOSITE ABOVE: Smoking a sheesha in Luxor market.
OPPOSITE BELOW: Fez souk.

Another striking feature of traditional Berber architecture is a type of granary known as a *ksar* (plural *ksour*), which is comprised of row upon row of semi-rectangular storage cells that stand up to five storeys high and resemble an outsized, surrealistic honeycomb. Despite their futuristic and otherworldly appearance, many of the region's larger *ksour* were built in mediaeval times and have been used by desert nomads as grain stores ever since. Sadly, most have fallen into disuse over recent years, though some *ksour* have been granted a new lease of life as curio markets or even hotels servicing an ever-growing tourist industry – and several were used as sets during the making of *Star Wars* and its sequels and prequels.

By comparison with the *ksour* of the southern countryside, the cities of the Maghreb have an overtly Arabian character. This dates back to the conquest of present-day Tunisia and the foundation of the city of Kairouan by the Islamic General Uqba ibn Nafi in AD 670. At the core of such venerable and atmospheric cities as Tunis, Algiers, Sfax, Marrakech, Fez, Rabat and Casablanca stand the old walled *medinas*. *Medina* is the Arabic word for a town or city and in North Africa refers to the central part of the city. The *medina* is named after the oasis that gave refuge to the Prophet Mohammed following his flight from Mecca in AD 622. The typical *medina* is enclosed by tall fortified stone walls with turrets, watchtowers and buttresses that betray their defensive origins. It can be entered via anything from two to half-a-dozen gates, the most important of which are normally arched and sealed by elaborately decorated wooden doors.

Run through by a labyrinth of narrow, shady alleys and hemmed in by tall rows of double- or triple-storey homesteads and caravanserais, most North African *medinas* come across as rather chaotic, with a haphazard design. In reality, however, the layout of every *medina* follows a religiously inspired design patented in the Arabian Gulf in the earliest days of Islam. The physical and spiritual focal point of urban life in the Maghreb is the Great Mosque, which is traditionally situated at the precise centre of the *medina* (though in some instances its relative location has shifted following modifications to the shape of the city walls), and is also generally the largest and most ostentatious building within it.

Adjacent to the Great Mosque, the main market area of the *medina* comprises several distinct *souks* – clusters of shops that specialize in a specific product or trade. The most holy items, such as prayer candles and religious books, are sold closest to the mosque. By contrast, less exalted artisans such as ironmongers and blacksmiths ply their trades immediately within the city walls, while the potentially malodorous likes of vegetable vendors and tanners are traditionally expected to operate outside of the *medina*. A *medina* usually contains several distinct residential quarters, each of which has its own public bath or *hammam*, as well as a few dozen private houses consisting of two or three storeys of rooms built around a closed central courtyard.

The urban Islamic architectural tradition of the Maghreb and its more rustic Berber counterpart converge on the small island of Djerba, which has been connected to the Tunisian mainland by a stone causeway since Roman times and is often cited as the legendary Land of the Lotus Eaters. Djerba has long been something of a cultural melting pot, having been occupied at various times by the Phoenicians, the Romans, the Normans, the Spanish and several Islamic sects. Despite these intrusions it remains predominantly Berber in feel, and forms the main North African stronghold for the Ibadite Muslims and Tunisia's small Jewish population. The semi-subterranean fortified houses or *menzels* that dot the Djerban countryside reflect a history of military invasions. Even more striking, perhaps, are the island's 200-odd fortress-like mosques. Indeed, these earthy, erratically shaped whitewashed buildings, distinguished by their thick, buttressed outer walls and squat minarets, come across as the architectural precursors to the adobe mosques of the Sahel.

BELOW: A traditional Islamic door in the *medina* of the Tunisian town of Hammamet.
BOTTOM: A twelfth-century fortress and cemetery overlook Hammamet's fishing harbour.

Roman Africa

According to legend, the city of Carthage, which lies on the same bay as present-day Tunis, was founded by the Tyrean Princess Elyssa (or Dido) in 814 BC. The Carthaginian Empire rose to become the dominant power in the southern Mediterranean, a position it enjoyed practically unchallenged until 264 BC, when Rome reversed a 250-year-old alliance to launch the first of three wars that would culminate in the razing of Carthage in 146 BC.

The sacking of Carthage was the first step in a process that took off in earnest after Julius Caesar defeated Pompey near the modern Tunisian port of Mahdia in 46 BC. Within 15 years, the entire North African coastal belt from the Nile to the Atlantic had been formally incorporated into the Roman Empire, and the reconstruction of Carthage to conform to a Roman design was under way.

Resistance to Roman rule soon gave way to political assimilation: AD 69 saw the appointment of the first African to the senate, and by AD 200 – the peak of the Golden Age of Roman Africa – up to a quarter of Roman senators were of North African origin. The decline in Roman influence can be dated to the late third century, which is also when Christianity first started to assert itself in North Africa. The capture of Carthage by a Germanic tribe called the Vandals in AD 439 sounded the death knell for Roman occupation. Christianity also proved to be ephemeral, its influence curtailed by the Arab invasions of the late seventh and eighth centuries, and the associated growth of Islam.

The Romans left behind some fine ruins in North Africa, none more so than the immense amphitheatre at El Jem. Aesthetically, however, Roman Africa is best known for having produced the most extensive and finest mosaic work of the period, with a strong thematic emphasis on the decadent god Dionysus or Bacchus, as well as on animals – local (lions), exotic (bears) and mythical (centaurs). Much of this mosaic work can be seen *in situ*, but many of the best panels are displayed in Tunis's superb Bardo Museum.

ABOVE: This second-century mosaic of a nymph on a seahorse was uncovered at the Tunisian town of El Jem.
BELOW: The coliseum of El Jem dates back to AD 230.
OPPOSITE: The forum at Sbeitla.

An ocean of sand

THE SAHARA DESERT

Extending for some 4 500 kilometres between the Atlantic coastline of Mauritania and the shores of the Red Sea, the Sahara is the world's largest desert, a practically unin-habitable barrier of extreme aridity dividing the ancient Sahelian trade outposts of Timbuktu and Agadez from the narrow belt of relative fertility fringing the Mediterranean. With almost 30 per cent of its area comprised of sandy dunes, known locally as *ergs*, and the remainder of rockier landscapes, the Sahara has existed in more-or-less its present form for about five million years. Prior to that, the same land lay closer to the equator and supported a moister, more wooded cover – indeed, it is thought that the first primates evolved about 50 million years ago in what was then a belt of equatorial rainforest rising from the present-day Sahara.

Inhospitable though it may be, the Sahara has been plied by Berber and Arabic traders since at least 3 000 years ago, when the first caravan route was established between Ghat in the south of present-day Libya and the port of Gao on the eastern Niger in present-day Mali. At first, trade was limited by the need to carry goods across the desert in horse-drawn chariots, but that changed with the introduction of camels – which need less water than horses and can carry a heavier load – to North Africa about 2 000 years ago. The caravan trade reached its peak in the late mediaeval era, when northbound items such as gold, kola nuts and slaves were bartered for salt mined in the heart of the Sahara, but it faded away gradually following the Portuguese establishment of a maritime trade route with the Gulf of Guinea.

The ancestors of the Berbers who facilitated the desert trade are the Tuareg: nomadic cameleers who inhabit the western Sahara from Mauritania to Niger. The Tuareg date their lineage back to a fourth-century queen called Tin Hanin, whose fabulously wealthy mausoleum in the Hoggar Mountains was excavated in 1927. Characteristically pale-skinned and ascetic in appearance, the Tuareg are also sometimes called the Blue People, a reference to the trademark blue robes worn by the men and the dye that often rubs off onto their skins.

The Sahara has not been uniformly arid over its five-million-year existence. On the contrary, its climate is cyclic, and it has experienced infrequent short periods of relatively generous precipitation, the most recent of which peaked 5 000 to 10 000 years ago. The rich outdoor gallery of Neolithic rock art that is spread across mountain ranges in Algeria, Niger, Libya and other countries is testimony to the fact that the Sahara then supported a cover of grassland savanna, not dissimilar to that found in drier parts of East Africa today. It also supported large mammal species such as elephant, giraffe, white rhinoceros and a now-extinct species of giant buffalo.

OPPOSITE: Tuareg cameleers, dressed in traditional blue robes, ride across the tall dunes of the Erg Chebbi in the Moroccan Sahara.
TOP: Tea is prepared with great ceremony by the Taureg of the Sahara.
ABOVE: Desert beetles of the Tenebrionid family live in sand dunes.

The Sahara forms a somewhat less attractive habitat to grazers today, but it does support a surprising variety of predators, notably Africa's greatest diversity of true foxes. The sand fox is the only canid endemic to the Sahara and Sahel fringe, but this desert also forms the main centre of population for the tiny, wide-eared fennec and the jackal-like Rüppell's fox, all of which also occur in the Arabian deserts, while the Nile Valley and Sinai Peninsula support a peripheral population of the thickly furred royal fox and the Mediterranean fringe harbours a low density of the European red fox. The cheetah is the only large feline to range into the desert proper, but some rocky areas close to oases still harbour elusive populations of leopard, and the Sahara supports Africa's only population of the rather lynx-like sand cat.

Several of Africa's most rare antelope species are endemic to the arid habitats of the Sahara and Sahel. The most threatened of these species is the scimitar-horned oryx, the official status of which was changed from 'Critically Endangered' to 'Extinct in the Wild' in 1998 – though it is faintly possible that small numbers still occur in remote parts of Chad and Niger. Fortunately, some 4 000-odd scimitar-horned oryx survive in captivity, and a reintroduction programme in northern Senegal has met with limited success. Another Critically Endangered species, with, at most, 500 wild individuals left in Mauritania, Mali and Niger, is the addax, which resembles an oryx with spiralled rather than decurved horns. It is probably the most truly desert-adapted of all antelopes. Two Sahara-Sahelian gazelle species are listed as Endangered: about 1 000 slender-horned gazelle remain, centred on Niger, while a similar number of dama gazelle have their main stronghold in Niger and Mali.

Camels

The ancient traders of the Sahara referred to it as the 'ship of the desert', while the Koran states that 'The Almighty in making animals created nothing preferable'. Others have been less kind – 'like a horse designed by a committee' is one famous description of its absurd, knock-kneed appearance. But the 160 different Arabic words that exist to describe it are sufficient testament to the singularity of the camel.

The Camelidae family evolved in North America about 45 million years ago, when forms as small as a rabbit and as tall as an elephant existed. Six species, rather more uniform in size, are recognized today. There are four hump-less South American varieties and two humped Old World ones. Of the latter, only the two-humped Bactrian camel persists in the wild, with fewer than 1 000 individuals left roaming the inhospitable Gobi Desert in Mongolia.

The one-humped Arabian camels or dromedaries have been domesticated and are more numerous. At least 10 million inhabit Arabia and North Africa. The Arabian camel might have been custom-made as a beast of burden suited to desert conditions: it has the capacity to travel 100 kilometres daily, bearing a load of up to 200 kilograms. Superficial desert adaptations include splayed feet for walking on sand, closable nostrils, and a double row of long eyelashes for protection in sandstorms. A camel can eat just about any vegetable matter, from grass and leaves to thorns and bark, and will also forage off carrion and bones. The hump stores fat, which can also be drawn upon for sustenance.

Most remarkable is the camel's capacity to survive for weeks without water. Sweat is minimal, the kidneys produce paste-like urine, and the faeces are so dry that they can be used for fuel immediately. During long periods without drinking, a camel can lose up to one-third of its weight by recycling water stored in the body tissues. At the end of an enforced fast it can gulp down more than 100 litres of water in 10 minutes, the dehydrated tissues immediately absorbing the moisture.

Camels can go for up to a week without food and water. Their feet have broad leathery pads which spread to prevent them sinking into the sand.

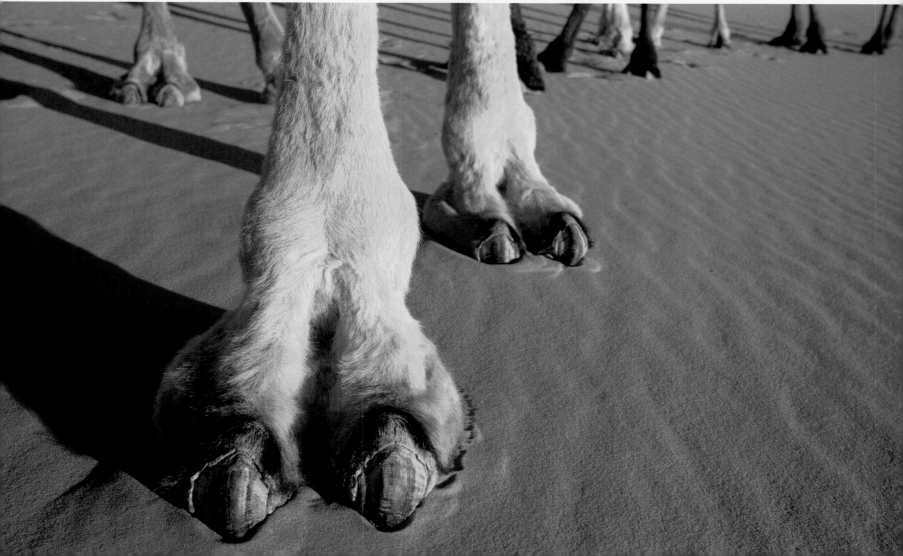

WEST AFRICA

Heading westward from the Congolese border with Tanzania and Uganda, the giddying natural variety that characterizes eastern and southern Africa gives way to an altogether more uniform landscape: a belt of low-lying rainforest that sprawls across the borders of almost 20 different countries before it peters out in Senegal and The Gambia. This is the Africa of Tarzan rather than the Lion King, of Conrad rather than Blixen; a swathe of verdant fertility whose steamy 'Heart of Darkness' – the incomprehensibly vast Congo Basin – remains almost as undeveloped and impenetrable as it was a century ago.

The Congo Basin and Guinean coast of West Africa together account for almost 30 per cent of the world's rainforest, and boast a level of terrestrial biodiversity second only to the Amazon Basin. Extending over two million square kilometres, the Congo Basin remains the vastest and least compromized of African wilderness areas. However, a recent increase in logging activity threatens to make the sort of incursion that reduced the area of the Guinean forests from more than one million to less than 200 000 square kilometres over the course of the twentieth century.

Undoubtedly, rainforest – interspersed with small moist grassy depressions known as bias – is the dominant motif in the West Africa landscape. But as one heads further north into Mali, Burkina Faso and Niger, the jungle thins out, to be replaced by the dry Sahelian acacia scrub on the southern verge of the Sahara – an arid landscape coursed through by some of Africa's most impressive rivers, including the Niger, Senegal and Volta.

West Africa supports diverse cultures, ranging from the hunter-gatherer Pygmies of the Congolese rainforest, to the sophisticated urbanites of the Ashanti Empire, from the animist Dogon of the Bandiagara Escarpment

OPPOSITE: A traditional fisherman plies his trade on the Dzanga River, Central African Republic.

69

to the ascetic Islamic camel herders of the Sahara fringe. It also boasts some of the continent's most haunting architecture, including curvaceous West Sudanese-style adobe buildings, which are scattered through the Sahel, and the magnificent mud-and-stick mosques that adorn the extant mediaeval trading centres of Djenné and Timbuktu.

More than any other part of the continent, the mosaic of small Anglophone and Francophone countries that occupy the so-called Bulge of Africa is where the distinction between traditional and contemporary culture becomes decidedly blurred. For this

BELOW: Lush rainforest blankets much of the Congolese Basin and Gulf of Guinea.

reason perhaps, West Africa has played a prominent role in the fusion of indigenous and exotic elements that characterizes many modern African art and craft forms, from sculpture and painting to drama and literature. Nowhere is this more apparent, however, than in the music, which incorporates jittery Ghanaian 'highlife' and jazzy Nigerian 'Afrobeat', both of which peaked in popularity in the 1960s, as well as the dazzling guitar work of contemporary Congolese pop, slick Latino productions of Senegalese disco, and haunting blues-like Arabic dirges from Mali.

BELOW: The chimpanzee is one of numerous primate species associated with the West African rainforest. CENTRE: A Dogon carving. BOTTOM: A fetish priest of the Ashanti Kingdom.

71

Ashanti

Founded in around 1690, the Ashanti Kingdom was the most powerful state ever to emerge in the pre-colonial Guinean interior – a region described by John Reader as 'the only part of Africa whose inhabitants found both mineral and agricultural resources in abundant quantities'.

With a sphere of influence that extended from modern-day Ghana into Côte d'Ivoire, Togo and Burkina Faso, Ashanti was the last and most enduring of a succession of centralized states that controlled the goldmines of Obuasi – a source of gold since mediaeval times. Gold is Ghana's number one export today. Unlike the empires that had preceded it, however, Ashanti did not export its gold, but rather stockpiled it. The Ashanti also stockpiled firearms accumulated by bartering the ample supply of captives that were taken during frequent military campaigns with coastal slave traders.

The capital of Ashanti, Kumasi was by all accounts an attractive and architecturally distinctive city before the British razed it in 1876. Today, by contrast, it is a seething urban sprawl of hawkers and traffic jams belying the epithet of 'Ancient Ashanti Capital'. Yet some fine examples of traditionall Ashanti architecture do exist, among them the 300-year-old fetish shrine at Besease, which is still in use today. Here, the queen mother Yaa Asantewaa consulted the spirits in 1901, before leading an ill-fated attack on the British fort at Kumasi.

Ashanti is renowned for its craftspeople. There are the weavers of Bonwire, who use traditional looms to make the region's trademark geometric kente cloth, and have received royal patronage since the reign of the first Ashanti king. Another popular cloth is adinkra, a plain white textile decorated with up to 60 different symbols – each signifying a specific tradition or proverb – and imprinted with calabash stamps and dyed using boiled tree-bark.

On every sixth Sunday, the Ashanti King sits in session at Kumasi's Manhyia Palace. Lesser chiefs assemble there to pay homage, some dressed in the finest adinkra, others in leopard, serval and other animal skins. The king's arrival is heralded by a procession of local dignitaries and royalty, while a fanfare of exuberant drumming and traditional horns captures some of the pageantry of the Ashanti past.

ABOVE: *A brass-smith at work in a village outside Kumasi.*
BELOW: *A traditional Kente cloth weaver at work.*
OPPOSITE: *The King of Ashanti holds court at Manhyia Palace.*

TIMBUKTU AND THE SAHEL

Transitional to the parched emptiness of the Sahara and the steamy Guinean rainforest, the arid savanna region known as the Sahel – an Arabic word meaning 'edge' – is a tough and unforgiving place. Dry and infertile at the best of times, the Sahel is also prone to regular rainfall failures, and can be intolerably hot and dusty. At the height of the hot *harmattan* winds, the effect is rather like being assaulted by an overgrown hairdryer in a sandpit.

Between the fifth and fifteenth centuries, a succession of powerful indigenous empires – Ougadou, Ghana, Mali and Songhay – presided over the Sahel. They thrived on the trans-Saharan trade in gold, ivory, kola nuts, slaves and salt. Pivotal to these ancient trade routes was the legendary city of Timbuktu, not the byword for obscurity it is today, but a thriving centre of Islamic scholarship and trade, perched on the junction of the Saharan caravan routes and the natural trade highway that is the Niger River.

Founded in the eighth century AD, Timbuktu was the urban funnel through which practically all trade between the Arab world and West Africa had to pass. As a measure of its mediaeval wealth, it is said that when the King of Timbuktu visited Mecca, his casually bestowed gifts undermined the local gold market for decades afterwards! Timbuktu's importance probably peaked in the fifteenth and sixteenth centuries, when the Arab traders who led their camels there from the Mediterranean regarded it as the caravan terminus at the edge of the universe, literally the end of the world as they knew it.

Timbuktu's decline can be traced to 1591, when it was captured by Morocco, an event from which neither it nor the trans-Sahara trade route would ever fully recover – though the fate of the latter was probably already sealed by the growing maritime trade between Europe and the coast of present-day Ghana. But oddly, even as these trade routes fell into decline, so Timbuktu grew in repute, its name resonating through the centuries to become a holy grail of European exploration. Today, no other phrase quite evokes the same sense of absenteeism as this: Going to Timbuktu.

Overshadowed by its history and visibly losing ground to the shifting Sahara sands, Timbuktu superficially contrives to feel like less than the sum of its parts. In 1828, when Rene Caillie became the first European to reach the fabled city and live to tell the tale, he noted that 'it was neither as big nor as populated as I expected ... I was amazed by the lack of energy, by the inertia'. More recently, the Irish singer Bob Geldof visited Timbuktu, took a quick look around, and asked simply: 'Is that it?'

OPPOSITE: Local Peul villagers arrive at Djenné by boat to attend the Monday market.
BELOW: Local fishermen in Djenné take advantage of the annual flooding of the seasonal tributary of the Niger.

Relics of Timbuktu's
former prominence
include the ornate
thirteenth-century mosque
(ABOVE LEFT AND RIGHT),
and thousands of
illuminated mediaeval
manuscripts (RIGHT)
housed in the UNESCO-
funded Cedrab library.

Yet Timbuktu is also curiously compelling, with a presence that grows over a few days' exploration. Its original thirteenth-century mosque has retained the organic beauty characteristic of the West Sudanese style, while the equally earthy Sankore Mosque, once the most important university in sub-Saharan Africa, still stands next to the market. But it is the UNESCO-funded Centre de Documentation et de la Recherche Ahmed Baba (Cedrab) Foundation, with its collection of 15 000 mediaeval manuscripts, that most fully evokes Timbuktu's elusive mystique. Here visitors realize that centuries before Dias circled the Cape or Shakespeare penned his first play, this sleepy Sahelian backwater was a centre of learning with few peers anywhere in the world.

The adobe architectural style associated with the Sahel reaches its apex on the walled island city of Djenné, which lies on a southern tributary of the Niger. Recently proclaimed a World Heritage Site in recognition of its astonishing level of architectural integrity and cohesion, Djenné is everything Timbuktu ought to be – a warren of narrow alleys lined with multistorey buildings constructed entirely from wood and clay using techniques developed in the fifteenth century.

BELOW: The hard angles of this imposing organic architectural style contrast greatly with the more curvaceous styles employed elsewhere in the Sahel.

Life in Djenné revolves around the Konboro Mosque, which towers above the marketplace like a surrealist sandcastle. The largest mud construction in the world, Konboro is also a strong contender for the accolade of Africa's most beautiful building. This gloriously rounded structure has a pleasingly symmetrical design, complemented by a smooth clay texture that glows warmly beneath the harsh Sahelian sun. On Mondays, when this superb mosque forms the backdrop to a market that attracts thousands of rural Malians from outlying villages, the scene suggests a Sahelian market as it must have been in the Middle Ages.

Just as the Konboro Mosque stands in defiant contrast to the bleak, windswept angularity of the Sahelian landscape, so too do its people. The Peul, also known as the Fula, are perhaps the archetypal Sahelian people. Pastoralists and traders by tradition, and almost exclusively Islamic in faith, they form an important minority group not only in Mali but also in Senegal and The Gambia. Peul women are particularly well known for adorning themselves with bright dresses, cumbersome traditional gold earrings, nose rings and mulberry-stain lip tattoos.

Most of the finest Sahelian architecture is found in Mali, but several stylistically similar whitewashed mosques are dotted around northern Ghana and Burkina Faso, most of them reckoned to be around 500 years old. The Palace of the Wa-Na in the town of Wa, although it was built in the nineteenth century, is a fine example of the whitewashed Ghanaian style, as is the much older mosque at Larabanga near the entrance to Mole National Park.

While the mediaeval empire of Mali was perhaps the wealthiest state ever to have evolved in West Africa, its modern namesake is one of the world's poorest countries. This has less to do with the stereotypical African *malaise* of corruption and mismanagement than with an endemic aridity exacerbated in recent years by creeping desertification. Yet Mali remains among the most proud and staunchly traditionalist of African nations, one where the diverse modern cultures all boast a strong identity and history stretching back to the glory days of Timbuktu.

OPPOSITE: A Koran school in the alleys of Djenné. ABOVE: A Peul woman carries firewood – a scarce commodity in the Sahel. OVERLEAF: Djenné's Konboro mosque, the finest example of Sahelian architecture in existence, is lent an added dimension by the colourful market which is held in front of it every Monday.

THIS PAGE AND OPPOSITE: Peul women are known for their colourful dresses, purple lip-dye, nose-rings, and heavy, ornate traditional earrings crafted from solid gold.

OVERLEAF: The Grand Mosque in Bobo-Dioulasso is probably the largest extant traditional building in Burkina Faso.

Enchanted escarpment
DOGON COUNTRY

Despite being surrounded on all sides by Islamic cultures, the Dogon people of Mali are the archetypal African animists, the name given to those who attribute spiritual qualities and consciousness to various inanimate objects and natural phenomena. And, as seen through the enchanted eyes of its inhabitants, the rocks and trees of the Bandiagara Escarpment – the 300-metre-high geological backbone of Dogon country – are practically a living entity, filled with all manner of troublesome genies, fetish shrines and taboos.

The burnished cliffs of the 150-kilometre-long escarpment are pockmarked with ancient cave dwellings excavated perhaps 1 000 years before the Dogon arrived in the area. Oral tradition attributes these excavations to the Tellem, a tribe of placid hunter-gatherer Pygmies who could transform into giants or grow wings when an emergency required them to reach the safety of their cliff dwellings. The caves doubled as tombs, a tradition that has been assimilated by the Dogon, who hoist their dead to a final resting place in the old Tellem excavations using rope manufactured from baobab fibres.

The Dogon believe that the souls of the dead find eventual refuge in a paradisaical ancestral land. Before that happens, however, they might spend years lurking around their former home, jealous of the fun being had by their living kin, and occasionally stirring a spot of mischief in revenge. The dead remain in this purgatorial state until the village holds its next Dama festival, a kind of communal spiritual cleansing exercise in which the souls of the dead are led away by masked and stilted dancers to rest eternally in the land of the ancestors. The Dama is the second most important event in the Dogon calendar, superseded only by the once-in-a-lifetime Sigi, which represents the renewal of the universe and is next due in 2027.

OPPOSITE: A Dogon woman grinds millet at Songo above the Bandiagara Escarpment.
BELOW: Abandoned Dogon cliff dwellings at the base of the Bandiagara Escarpment.

LEFT, BELOW AND OPPOSITE: Elaborately masked *awa* dancers perform at a Dama festival in Ireli. Held annually in May, this most important of the Dogon festivals serves as a communal spiritual cleansing exercise. OVERLEAF: Interspersed with conical, thatched granaries, the flat roofs of a typical Dogon village are used for sleeping and drying grain and other fresh produce.

The Dogon villages that nestle along the escarpment are fantastic hobbit-warrens of flat-roofed adobe dwellings and conical granaries that seem to mushroom organically from between the baobabs and boulders. The villages have an anthropomorphic layout: the Toguna or Casa Palaver symbolizes the head: the low-roofed, open-sided building where men convene to relax and to hold communal meetings.

Each Dogon compound is also designed to symbolize the human body. The entrance is decorated with carvings that represent both male and female genitalia, echoing a Dogon belief that children are born with twin souls, one of each sex, with the secondary twin manifesting itself physically as the clitoris or foreskin. As in many African societies, the most important rite of passage is the circumcision ceremony, which is held tri-annually at Songo, below a rock overhang decorated with hundreds of paintings of animals such as pythons and jackals – the latter being the most revered of creatures, and in direct communication with the creator Amma.

The most powerful spiritual leader in a Dogon community, the *hogon* is the only person able to communicate with a serpentine deity called Lebe, who is said to lick his earthly medium's skin every night in order to keep him pure. Because Lebe is associated with climatic conditions and agriculture, the *hogon* officiates over all agricultural ceremonies, and he is also called upon to make sacrifices to Lebe in times of drought.

BELOW: Mass Dogon circumcision ceremonies are held tri-annually at Songo, below a rock overhang adorned with hundreds of paintings of sacred animals and a variety of cryptic patterns and abstractions.

OPPOSITE: The *hogon* is the most powerful spiritual leader in any Dogon community.

For 500 years prior to the colonial era, the Dogon suffered intermittent persecution at the hands of nomadic slave raiders as well as the Islamic communities that hem them in. To protect against such attacks, many Dogon villages along the falaise (escarpment) were built at the highest point that was accessible without rope. Colonialism granted the Dogon relative immunity from such attacks, and by 1930 many people had abandoned their cramped cliff-side dwellings to spread out onto the plains next to their fields.

The Dogon villages have lost a few metres in altitude over the past century, many have been infused with Islam or Christianity, and a few have been subjected to quite remarkable seasonal influxes of tourists. Even so, a surreal, insular mood pervades Dogon country. Visitors are expected to enter it on Dogon terms, sleeping as the locals do, on a roof-top mat loomed over by the majestic cliffs of the falaise and the many dozens of generations of Dogon ancestors that lie entombed within them.

BELOW: Abandoned Dogon cliff dwellings overlook the village of Teli, at the base of the Bandiagara Escarpment.

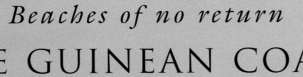

Beaches of no return

THE GUINEAN COAST AND RAINFOREST

The Dahomey Gap, a 200-kilometre-wide strip of savanna centred on Benin and Togo, divides the verdant swathe of forest centred on the Congo Basin from the belt of equatorial rainforest that follows the Bulge of Africa west from Ghana to Gambia via Côte d'Ivoire, Liberia, Sierra Leone, Guinea and southern Senegal. Known as the Upper Guinea Forest Block, this most westerly of Africa's evergreen forests receives less rainfall than its Congolese counterpart. It is also far patchier as a result of intensive logging over the past 10 years, as well as clearance for agriculture, settlement, plantation development and mining. Nevertheless, the Guinean Rainforest Belt – which also includes the transitional forest running east from the Dahomey Gap to western Cameroon – is ranked among the world's top 25 biodiversity hotspots, and is the most diverse in terms of mammals, with more than 550 species recorded.

The Dahomey Gap has long formed a natural obstacle between Africa's two largest rainforest blocks, with the result that several species are restricted to one or other side. For example, the Dahomey Gap appears to have blocked the westward expansion of the gorilla, forest otter and swamp monkey, while the likes of Jentink's and zebra duiker, Diana monkey, Brown-cheeked Hornbill and White-breasted Guineafowl are all endemic to the Upper Guinea Forest Block. Likewise, distinct racial populations of at least six forest primates, including pied colobus and mona monkey, occur on either side of the gap.

Poaching for bush meat has hit the indigenous wildlife of the Guinean rainforest very hard, and – except in formal wildlife sanctuaries – there are now many places where the only large animals to survive are those considered taboo by local villagers. Even those forests that are officially protected as national parks or forest reserves tend to receive a far lower level of on-the-ground attention than their counterparts in East and southern Africa. Fortunately, the very inaccessibility of the rainforest interior provides a greater degree of intrinsic protection than more open habitats.

Once teeming with plains game, the belt of wooded savanna dividing the Guinean rainforest from the arid Sahel is possibly the most compromised African eco-zone. The region has witnessed several extinctions of fauna in recent years, most notably perhaps black rhino, while local races of giant eland, giraffe, and African hunting dog seem to be headed the same way. The only hope for the region's savanna elephant and lion populations is the clutch of under-funded national parks, of which the most prominent are probably Mole in Ghana, Niakolo-Koba in Senegal, and d'Arli in Burkina Faso.

OPPOSITE: The Castle of St George in Elmina, Ghana, founded by the Portuguese in 1482, is the oldest European building in sub-Saharan Africa. BELOW: The mona monkey is a common resident of the Guinean rainforest.

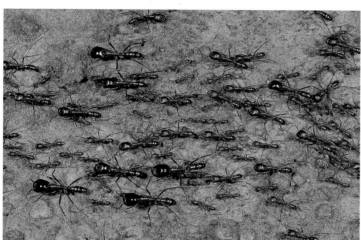

OPPOSITE: Forest elephants gather to drink at a *bai* – a grassy clearing containing a watering hole.

ABOVE LEFT: Butterflies of the famlies Pieridae and Lycaenidae gather at mineral and salt deposits in the tropical rainforest.

ABOVE RIGHT: The Senegal parrot adds a dash of colour to the belt of semi-arid savanna that divides the Guinean rainforest from the Sahel.

LEFT: Army ants, living in colonies of up to 20 million, march in predatory unison across the rainforest floor.

BELOW: The endangered dwarf crocodile is endemic to rainforest pools and rivers in western and central Africa.

Deforestation and bush meat

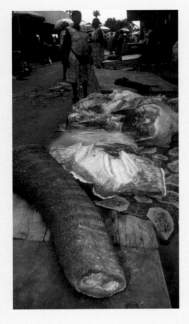

Of all Africa's non-arid wilderness areas, the endless jungle that sprawls across the Congo Basin was, until recently, the least affected by the wholesale slaughter of plains wildlife that is associated with the arrival of European firearms. Since the early 1990s, however, the wildlife that inhabits this remote rainforest ecosystem has come under increasing pressure from a variety of threats. This has been spearheaded by the increased incidence of illegal or uncontrolled logging in areas of pristine rainforest formerly inhabited by a low density of Pygmy hunter-gatherers.

The most direct consequence of logging – most of which is undertaken by European concerns – is the loss of centuries-old hardwood resources for a minimal return. More serious, however, is the cutting of roads into virgin territory, which tends to attract fresh human settlement and the clearance of forest for cultivation. The twin menaces of logging and subsistence farming are thought to be depleting the Congo Basin forests by 0,6 per cent annually – at which rate one-fifth of the region's forests could be gone by the year 2020.

Logging roads also open up tracts of undisturbed forest to commercial hunters, who are believed to have shifted more than a million tons of bush meat to the towns and cities of the Congo Basin in 2003, most of it transported by passing logging trucks. It has been estimated that in the Democratic Republic of Congo alone, some 500 gorillas are poached annually for bush meat, and the effect on chimpanzees – as well as smaller primates and forest antelope species – is similarly devastating. Indeed, at present rates of consumption, all of Africa's great apes are likely to be extinct within the next 50 years.

The main victims of the bush-meat trade are primates and antelope. But it also poses a threat to humans in the form of viral diseases. For example, HIV/Aids is very closely related to SIV, the simian immune virus, and is thought to have been transferred to the human population through monkeys used for food. Recent studies also indicate that isolated outbreaks of the deadly Ebola virus are linked to the consumption of infected primate meat.

ABOVE: Bush meat, including an elephant trunk, for sale at an urban market.
BELOW: Poached monkeys for sale by the roadside.
OPPOSITE ABOVE: A bulldozer clears vegetation from virgin forest in Gabon, allowing commercial hunters access.
OPPOSITE BELOW: Guards inspect an elephant killed by poachers.

The people of the Guinean rainforest established indirect trade links with the Mediterranean at least 1 500 years ago, when gold and kola nuts sourced from present-day Ghana and Côte d'Ivoire were transported via the Niger River to Timbuktu, then across the Sahara by Berber caravans. Trade become more direct after Portugal, having captured the Moroccan port of Ceuta in 1415, set about exploring the *terra incognito* to the south in order to locate the source of the Saharan gold. They hit the jackpot in 1471, when a Portuguese ship set anchor at Elmina (or, 'the mine'). The town of Elmina boasted a prodigious salt production centre, where the king – 'dressed with a golden collar of precious stones, legs and arms covered with golden bracelets and rings, and in his plaited beard golden bars' – had managed to establish good trade links with the inland goldfields.

Starting with the Portuguese construction of the Castle of St George at Elmina in 1482, half a dozen different European powers built an astonishing total of 80 forts along the so-called Gold Coast (essentially the Atlantic coast of modern Ghana), which historian Albert van Dantzig has referred to as 'the ancient shopping street of West

BELOW: Brightly painted fishing pirogues dot the lagoon below St George's Castle in Elmina.

Africa'. Throughout the fifteenth century, the Portuguese exported £100 000 of gold from West Africa annually – roughly 10 per cent of the global supply – thereby piquing the interest of several rival European powers. English ships first arrived in 1530, followed by the French 12 years later, but it was the Dutch that ended Portuguese tenure of the Gold Coast when they captured St George's Castle in 1637.

The castles and forts of Ghana are elevated from curiosity value to something altogether more potent and chilling by their role in the slave trade. Not that Ghana was especially active in this insidious practice – on the contrary, Portugal and later Holland outlawed the purchase of slaves on the Gold Coast, on the basis that it might destabilize the lucrative gold trade. However, it is one of the few places where the trade was conducted out of buildings of sufficient substance to have survived into the modern era. And in the late seventeenth century, England deliberately opted to undermine the Dutch monopoly by using Cape Coast Castle, 10 kilometres east of Elmina, as a base from which to buy slaves, leading one Dutch official to bemoan that 'the Gold Coast had changed into a virtual Slave Coast'.

BELOW: A rusting cannon on the ramparts of Fort Metal Cross overlooks the small fishing port of Dixcove.
OVERLEAF: Colourful boats in Elmina harbour.

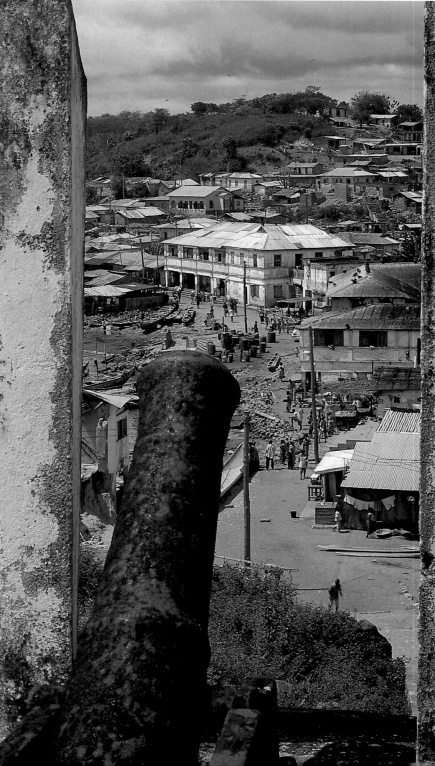

The Atlantic slave trade

The slave trade between West Africa and the Americas is a singular event in human history, not simply because it operated on an unprecedented scale, but also because it was so wide-ranging in its effects. Between the seventeenth and nineteenth centuries, up to 20 million West Africans were transported across the Atlantic, a five-week trip in conditions so cramped and unhygienic that up to half of a boat's captive passengers could die en route.

Often perceived to be an abomination introduced by Europeans, a slave trade had been in place since the earliest days of the trans-Saharan caravans, and slavery itself existed in most indigenous African societies. Before the arrival of Europeans, however, such slaves were typically incidental captives of war, and able to integrate into the society that enslaved them. By contrast, at the peak of the trans-Atlantic slave trade, the taking of captives had become the justification for war.

Most Westerners are familiar with the fate of the trade's victims. Rather less well documented is the devastating effect it had on African society. Traditional industries were lost as their products became almost worthless by comparison with slaves. An inter-tribal arms race built up and, in the seventeenth century, Britain alone supplied around 100 000 guns annually to West Africa. Furthermore, a high proportion of able-bodied Africans were lost, in exchange for items such as alcohol and tobacco – at best of no lasting value and at worst entirely destructive.

After the industrial revolution, the anti-slavery lobby became a powerful voice in Europe. In 1804, Denmark abolished the slave trade, followed by Britain in 1807, while several other governments signed a treaty allowing Britain to search boats captained by other nations – it became a common practice among slavers to throw their human cargo overboard at the approach of a British naval patrol. It was soon recognized that only by abolishing the use of slave labour would the trade be ended: Britain introduced abolition throughout its colonies in 1833, followed by France in 1848, the USA in 1865, and finally Brazil in 1888.

ABOVE AND OPPOSITE ABOVE:
The Fort of São Antonio, built in 1515, served as a Dutch slave-trading centre for several centuries.
BELOW: A painted panel at the former trading post of Aldebra in the Gambia.
OPPOSITE BELOW: Cape Coast Castle was the most important centre of the English slave trade.

As the former British and Dutch headquarters on the Gold Coast respectively, Cape Coast and Elmina castles have spent much of their history glowering at each other across the 10-kilometre stretch of palm-lined coastline that divides them. Both now operate as museums dedicated to the iniquities of the trans-Atlantic trade in African slaves. Cape Coast today is a lively university town of narrow roads and alleys lined with colonial-era buildings, whereas the more low-key Elmina – its harbour teeming with brightly painted pirogues – has returned to its fishing village roots, lending the castle that towers above it a sense of physical dislocation common to many of Ghana's old forts.

Arguably the most cohesive of West Africa's European relics is the small island of Gorée, whose proximity to the bustling Senegalese capital of Dakar – 15 minutes by ferry – belies a difference in mood that might be measured in centuries. The recorded history of Gorée is virtually as long as that of the European exploration of Africa itself. The Portuguese, who aptly but unimaginatively named it Ile de Palma, visited it in 1444 and its safe location in West Africa's largest sheltered bay made it popular with ships coming from Europe as a place to drop anchor. In 1588 the island fell to the Dutch, who renamed it Goede Reede, 'Good Harbour', which was corrupted to Gorée after the French occupation of 1677.

BELOW: Poling a dugout to the stilt village of Nzulezu in western Ghana.
OPPOSITE: Vibrant drumming lies at the heart of traditional West African music.

Gorée today doubles as sleepy fishing village and even sleepier resort town, popular not only with foreign tourists – recent visitors include Bill Clinton and Nelson Mandela – but also with Dakarois weekenders seeking a break from the city's relentless car horns. Too small to get lost on, Gorée is best explored whimsically, by randomly following any of its narrow, winding alleys until one chances upon one of the many architectural landmarks or museums. Its most famous building is the Maison des Esclaves, 'House of Slaves', built by the island's renowned *signaress* – women of mixed European and African parentage who founded important trade dynasties through their European connections – and notable architecturally for its curving double-crescent stairway. Now a museum, the building serves as a poignant reminder that Gorée, somnolent as it might be today, was once highly active in the slave trade: the entrance that leads from the dungeons to the rocky shore is known as the Door of No Return, in tribute to the hundreds of thousands of Africans who passed through it to be loaded onto an America-bound ship.

OPPOSITE: Attractive colonial architecture is a feature of Gorée Island, off the coast of Senegal.
BELOW: A poignant reminder of the slave trade, the Maison des Esclaves on Gorée Island has attracted several notable visitors, among them Bill Clinton and Nelson Mandela.

LEFT: Woven by the Ashanti and Ewe of Ghana, Kente cloth is one of the most striking fabrics produced in West Africa.

BELOW: A traditional Gambian dancer is surrounded by curious children in the streets of Banjul.

OPPOSITE: Brightly decorated adobe houses are a feature of villages in the Ghana-Burkina Faso border area.

OVERLEAF: The busy fishing market at the Senegalese port of Mbour.

Heart of greenness

THE CONGO BASIN

More than one-quarter of the world's remaining primary rainforest extends across the vast lowland basin drained by Africa's second-longest river, the wide and sluggish Congo, which runs for 4 375 kilometres from its source in the Albertine Rift to the Atlantic. This two-million square kilometre tract of sweltering jungle, exceeded in area only by South America's Amazon, is split between five countries, with roughly half of its area falling into the Democratic Republic of Congo (DRC), and the remainder divided between Cameroon, Central African Republic, Congo Republic and Gabon.

The most complex and – not coincidentally – the least understood of terrestrial ecosystems, rainforests typically thrive on a non-seasonal equatorial climate. Year-round high temperatures, precipitation and humidity collectively encourage an evergreen cover of tall trees forming a closed canopy. The Congo rainforest is rather unusual in that it has a defined dry season and contains a minority of deciduous flora, but its annual rainfall figure does exceed 1 500 millimetres, and the weather is reliably hot and sticky.

Thinly inhabited and largely inaccessible, the Congo ranks as one of the world's great biodiversity hotspots, with the DRC alone boasting 415 described mammal and 1 117 described bird species, the largest tallies for any African country. Several intriguing mammal species are confined to the Congo Basin, among them the golden cat, fishing genet, giant genet and water chevrotain. The chevrotain is an antelope-like relict of an ancient ungulate family, which shares several structural features with pigs and is regarded to be the ancestor of all modern-day bovids. Also peculiar to the Congo Basin is the okapi, a kudu-sized 'living fossil' first described as recently as 1900, and the only modern survivor of a formerly widespread genus of savanna browsers that are related to the giraffe.

Restricted to forested habitats south of the Congo River, the bonobo (or pygmy chimpanzee) is rather more lightly built than the common chimpanzee, and is possibly even more closely related to humans – certainly it is the only other primate to copulate face-to-face! Also unique to the Congo Basin are the endangered drill and the rainbow-faced mandrill, a pair of relatively terrestrial baboon-like primates whose mutually exclusive ranges are separated by the Sanaga River in southern Cameroon.

The Congo Basin boasts Africa's greatest wealth of arboreal monkeys, divided into two subfamilies, the thumbless colobines and cheek-pouched cercopithecines. The colobines, all but confined to rainforest habitats between latitudes of 12 degrees North and 12 degrees South, are easily distinguished from other African monkeys by their long tails, spidery limbs and rather slight frame. All colobines are strongly arboreal, and they subsist almost entirely on leaves and other leguminous matter processed by a somewhat ruminant-like digestive system.

OPPOSITE: The morning sun lights up a misty forest patch in the Central African Republic. BELOW: More lightly built and redder in colour than its familiar savanna counterpart, the forest buffalo is endemic to the rainforests of West and Central Africa.

OPPOSITE: A forest elephant in the Dzanga-Ndoki National Park in the Central African Republic uses its tusks and trunk to dig up mineral-rich mud to supplement its diet.

LEFT: As beautiful as it is venomous, a sedge viper coils to strike with an open mouth.

BELOW: Innumerable forest-fringed rivers run through the Congo Basin before draining into the mighty Congo River.

Pygmies

The most ancient of Africa's human rainforest dwellers, Pygmies – like the Bushmen of southern Africa – are distinguished from most other Africans by their slight stature, bronzed complexion and adherence to a hunter-gatherer lifestyle. Pygmies traditionally live in semi-nomadic communities whose lifestyle is based around hunting, undertaken as a team effort by the men. In some areas, the *modus operandi* involves part of the hunting party stringing a long net between a few trees, while the remaining party members advance noisily towards it to herd in small game. Elsewhere, poisoned arrows are favoured: the hunting party will shoot their target from a distance, wait until it drops, and then, if necessary, deliver the final blow with a spear.

Today, some 200 000 Pygmies inhabit the equatorial rainforest belt between Cameroon and the Albertine Rift, divisible into several localized subgroups, of which the Bambuti, with an average height of 1,25 metres, are the shortest of all human communities. Pygmies still pursue their traditional lifestyle in more remote parts of the Congo Basin, but elsewhere their freedom has been impinged upon greatly by logging companies, conservationists, commercial hunters and other outsiders. In western Uganda, for instance, some 80 per cent of the 2 000 remaining Batwa and Bambuti Pygmies are officially landless. They have no legal access to the forest on which their traditional livelihood depends, and other locals subject them to ridicule and occasional violence.

Anti-Pygmy prejudice is not confined to their immediate neighbours. Richard Nzita's otherwise commendable *People and Cultures of Uganda* contrives, in the space of two pages, to characterize the Batwa as beggars, crop raiders, pottery thieves and cannibals. Conservationists and the Western media, meanwhile, persistently and inaccurately stigmatize Pygmies as gorilla or chimpanzee hunters and poachers. This is despite the fact that their ancient lifestyle is a model example of the sustainable use of natural resources. Indeed, while Pygmies have played no significant role in the deforestation of equatorial Africa, they have certainly been the main human victims of the habitat loss to date.

The Baaka Pygmies of Cameroon and the Central African Republic are Africa's last remaining hunter-gatherers, feeding mainly on forest duikers and monkeys. They live in simple huts made of leaves and often spend evenings performing lively dances and songs.

The colobines have long been the subject of taxonomic debate. Two clear generic groupings are widely recognized, namely the red colobines, *Procolobus,* and pied colobines, *Colobus.* Of up to 20 recognized pied colobus taxa, it is only the black colobus, a unique all-black form found in Gabon and Cameroon, that is unambiguously a distinct species. The remainder are generally (although not universally) ascribed to three different species. Exactly how many species of red colobus range through Africa is more of an open question: between 30 and 40 taxa have been described, some probably intermediate forms rather than definable races, and as many as eight might be good species.

The cheek-pouch monkeys, of which the savanna-dwelling vervet monkey and common baboon are the most familiar representatives, are a far more varied bunch. Named for their characteristic inner-cheek pouches, which in many species can hold as much food as a full stomach, they occupy a wide range of ecological niches. This is particularly true of the guenons of the genus *Cercopithecus.* In addition to the savanna-dwelling vervet and patas monkeys, dozens of forest-associated *Cercopithecus* taxa are recognized, yet all but three – the Diana monkey, De Brazza's monkey and the owl-faced monkey – are normally ascribed to one of four superspecies: the mona, cephus, mitis and L'Hoest's monkeys.

The most widespread and complex of these superspecies is the mitis monkey, which embraces approximately 25 taxa that vary widely in appearance. This situation is further confused by a litany of common names used interchangeably around Africa, for example: blue monkey, samango monkey, diademed guenon, silver monkey, Syke's monkey, and gentle monkey. If you find all this rather confusing, so do the guenons! A number of reliable reports have come to light that document mitis and cephus taxa interbreeding to produce fertile offspring in two different national parks, and many species hybridize in captivity with ease!

Given the vast numbers of primate taxa which are distributed across Africa, it is remarkable that none have been declared extinct during the course of the twentieth century. The prognosis for the next 100 years is rather more bleak. Miss Waldron's red colobus, a distinctive race first collected in 1933, recently gained the dubious distinction of being the first primate to be declared 'probably extinct' in more than a century. However, there is some doubt as to the validity of this declaration, as it may be premature. A relict population is thought to persist in Ghana's little explored Krokosua Forest Reserve, but it does underline the threat posed to many forest monkeys. And it may well turn out that Miss Waldron's red colobus was beaten to the gong by the little-known Bouvier's red colobus, a Congolese race that hasn't been sighted in 30 years, possibly as a result of its inaccessible swampy habitat, but more probably because none remain to be seen.

In January 2000, Conservation International and the Primate Specialist Group of the World Conservation Union (IUCN) released a joint report which highlighted 25 of the world's most immediately endangered primates. The seven African primates listed included two races of gorilla, along with four West and Central African monkey taxa: the aforementioned Miss Waldron's red colobus, the white-naped mangabey, the drill and Sclater's monkey. Sclater's monkey, a diminutive guenon first described from a zoo specimen in 1904 and rediscovered in the wild 84 years later, is regarded as the rarest of African primate species, with no more than a few thousand individuals remaining in areas of swampy forest between the Cross and Niger river deltas in Nigeria. The most concerning aspect of this shortlist is the number of extremely localized and vulnerable primates that are omitted – as many as one-third of Africa's higher primate taxa face a short- to medium-term threat of extinction.

OPPOSITE: The range of the endangered mandrill is restricted to Cameroon and Gabon. The males have distinctive, brightly coloured masks in order to display sexual fitness. BELOW: The attractive moustached monkey is endemic to the rainforests of the Congo Basin.

Gorillas

The largest living primates, and among the most peaceable, gorillas are widespread residents of the equatorial African rainforest. All gorillas are conventionally assigned to the same species, split into three main racial populations: the western lowland gorilla of the west-central Congo Basin, the eastern lowland gorilla of the eastern Congo Basin, and the mountain gorilla of the eastern Albertine Rift. However, recent DNA tests have led many experts to regard western and eastern lowland gorillas as genetically distinct as, for instance, humans and chimpanzees.

The two lowland races were described in the mid-eighteenth century, but the mountain gorilla remained unknown to science until 1902, when Oscar van Beringe shot two individuals in the Virunga Mountains. It was here too that George Schaller undertook the first study of gorilla behaviour in the 1950s, the starting point for the research programme initiated in Rwanda by Dian Fossey, author of the acclaimed *Gorillas in the Mist*.

Gorillas are sociable creatures, moving in defined troops comprised of a dominant 'silverback' male (the male's back turns silver when he reaches sexual maturity), a harem of mature females, and several youngsters. Unusually for mammals, the male forms the focal point of gorilla society. When a silverback dies, the troop normally disintegrates. Almost exclusively vegetarian, gorillas spend most of their day on the ground, retreating to the trees at night, when they build temporary nests. They are surprisingly sedentary creatures, typically moving less than one kilometre in a day, except after a stressful incident such as an aggressive encounter with another troop.

The status of the western lowland gorilla is reasonably secure, with more than 50 000 individuals left in the wild. Not so that of the eastern lowland gorilla, of which an estimated 15 000 remained prior to the ongoing war in the Democratic Republic of Congo, a figure that would be highly optimistic today. In 2000, the Cross River gorilla (*diehli*), a recently named race confined to the Cameroon-Nigeria border, and the mountain gorilla shared the dubious distinction of being placed on a shortlist of the world's 25 most endangered primate taxa.

*The endangered mountain gorilla (**ABOVE**) is restricted to 700 throughout two mountain ranges along the Albertine Rift, while the western lowland gorilla (**BELOW AND OPPOSITE**), though also endangered, is a far more common resident of lowland forests in the Congo Basin.*

EAST AFRICA

East Africa possesses an epic quality, a breathtaking natural largesse only hinted at by the geographical statistics. There is Lake Victoria, the largest lake in Africa, second largest in the world, and official source of the world's longest river. Further south is the 675-kilometre Lake Tanganyika – the longest and second deepest freshwater body on Earth. Kenya, Tanzania, Uganda, Rwanda and Ethiopia share all but one of the continent's 10 highest mountains; Kilimanjaro, the highest point in Africa, is also the tallest freestanding mountain in the world.

Then there are those peerless concentrations of wildlife, epitomized by the annual migration of up to two million wildebeest and zebra across Tanzania's Serengeti Plains, and the million-strong flocks of flamingos that aggregate on Kenya's Lake Nakuru and Lake Bogoria. In addition to the established safari favourites – lion, leopard, elephant, rhino, giraffe and various antelope species – are also the endangered mountain gorillas of misty Virunga, the celebrity chimps of Gombe Stream, and a rich variety of other forest primates. East Africa is also notable for its bird life – Kenya, Tanzania and Uganda each boast more than 1 000 species.

This landscape is dominated by the Great Rift Valley, a fissure so vast that it's the only terrestrial landmark visible from the moon. Some 25 million years ago, the Arabian and African tectonic plates started to slide apart. Present-day rifting activity in the region is a continuation of this same process, which caused the ancient monolithic landmass of Gondwanaland to break up into its present constituent parts some 200 million years ago, and which, more recently, set Madagascar adrift from the African mainland. Eventually – millions of years from now – the Great Rift Valley is likely to flood, transforming Africa as we know it into two or more separate landmasses.

OPPOSITE: A Lappet-faced Vulture surveys the wildebeest-studded grassland of the Maasai Mara in Kenya from atop an isolated acacia tree.

BELOW: *Relatively unaffected by poaching, Kenya's Amboseli National Park, set on the Tanzanian border below the distinctive snow-capped silhouette of Kilimanjaro, is known for its impressive tuskers.*

Far from being a straightforward linear fissure, the Rift Valley is actually Y-shaped, comprising three main axes that converge on the mountainous southeast of Tanzania. To outsiders, the most familiar of these axes is the Gregory Rift, which runs for more than 2 500 kilometres through the heart of Tanzania, Kenya and Ethiopia, and is named after the British geologist who first recognized it for what it is. Its archetypal East African cover of dry acacia scrubland has featured in countless documentaries and films. The southern axis of the Rift is most dramatic where it encloses the 585-kilometre-long Lake Malawi within a 1 000-metre-high escarpment, but it peters out somewhat as it follows the Shire River southward into the Zambezi Valley. The narrower and more clearly defined northwestern branch, which is known as the Albertine Rift, runs for

approximately 1 500 kilometres along the western borders of Tanzania, Burundi, Rwanda and Uganda, before dissipating near the Sudanese border north of Lake Albert.

The staggering scenic and natural abundance that characterize the eastern section of the continent is easily matched by the tremendous cultural diversity that embraces its many inhabitants: the relict hunter-gatherer Hadza and Batwa people, traditional pastoralists such as the Maasai and Borena, the Arab-tinged Swahili of the coast, the idiosyncratic Coptic-influenced Christians of the Ethiopian Highlands, the centralized kingdoms of Uganda and the cultural hotchpotch of South Omo ... not to mention the cosmopolitan, modern face of Africa that thrives in cities such as Nairobi, Kampala and Dar es Salaam.

BELOW: A Maasai girl with beaded jewellery. CENTRE: The black-and-white colobus monkey feeds exclusively on leaves. BOTTOM: Draped in colourful *vitenge* cloths, two Swahili girls chat in front of an old studded door on Zanzibar island.

129

Where East meets West

THE ALBERTINE RIFT

The western arm of the Rift Valley, which forms a rough crescent along the Congolese border with Tanzania, Burundi, Rwanda and Uganda, is, if anything, even more scenic than its eastern counterpart. Certainly, its high-altitude climate has bequeathed it a verdant sheen that contrasts strongly with the parched scrubland of the Ethiopian or Kenyan rifts. Four vast, serpentine lakes – Tanganyika, Kivu, Edward and Albert (the latter being the source of the term Albertine Rift) take up three-quarters of the valley floor. The remaining area supports a cover of rank grassland and lowland rainforest.

Protruding from the floor of the Albertine Rift, the Rwenzori is the largest mountain range in Africa, boasting five glacial peaks including the 5 109-metre Mount Stanley, named after the explorer credited with discovering the range. Stanley believed the Rwenzori to be the snow-capped 'Mountains of the Moon' cited by the Roman geographer Ptolemy as the source of the Nile. It is more likely that the 'Lunae Montes' Ptolemy had heard about described Mount Kilimanjaro or Mount Kenya, and that the relationship to the Nile was pure conjecture. Nevertheless, the association between the Rwenzori and the so-called Mountains of the Moon has proved enduring, and is unintentionally appropriate. The upper moorland – 'a world of fantasy where nothing is real but only a wild and lovely flight of imagination' according to Eric Shipton – does indeed possess a disarming, otherworldly quality.

Unique among East Africa's major peaks, the Rwenzoris are not volcanic in origin, though the surrounding area is dotted with at least 100 crater lakes, gem-like relicts of a spate of volcanic activity that peaked between 7 000 and 10 000 years ago. The Virungas provide somewhat more emphatic evidence of the volcanic activity associated with the rifting process: this chain consists of eight freestanding volcanic cones that rise from a fault line straddling the borders of Uganda, Rwanda and the Congo. Formed over the past two million years, the volcanoes all exceed 3 000 metres in altitude – indeed, Karisimbi (4 507 metres) and Mikeno (4 437 metres) are the sixth and seventh highest mountains in Africa.

OPPOSITE: A Congolese woman smokes her pipe below Mount Sabinyo, an extinct volcano whose peak marks the point where Uganda, Rwanda and the Democratic Republic of Congo converge.
BELOW: A taxi-boat ferries locals between ports on Lake Tanganyika.

Two of the Virunga cones remain highly volatile. Nyamuragira is probably the most active volcano on the African mainland, with 34 eruptions recorded since 1882, only one of which resulted in any fatalities. By contrast, Nyiragongo only erupted twice in the past century, but wreaked havoc on both occasions – an estimated 2 000 people were killed in 1977 by streams of molten lava that flowed at 60 kilometres per hour, while the 2002 eruption, which reached the Lake Kivu port of Goma, claimed at least 50 lives and left 12 000 families homeless.

Until about 200 years ago, the northern Albertine Rift escarpment was swathed in a continuum of rainforest so ancient that it had served as a vital refuge for numerous forest creatures during the Pleistocene Era when lower-lying areas such as the Congo Basin were afflicted by drought. The fragmentation of this forest started at the dawn of the Iron Age, when the first patches were cut down to make way for agriculture, and the process has accelerated over the last 100 years thanks to an ever-growing need for arable land. Today, perhaps a dozen viable relict forest patches remain on the eastern escarpment, the most substantial of which are protected within Rwanda's Nyungwe Forest Reserve and Uganda's Bwindi National Park, though neither compares in area to the extensively forested Itombwe Mountains on the western shore of Lake Tanganyika.

The Albertine Rift is one of the most significant biodiversity hotspots on the African mainland, with more than 1 100 endemic species described to date. This list includes a

BELOW: Rwanda's Nyungwe National Park protects the largest contiguous forest block in East Africa and forms the watershed between the drainage basins of Africa's two greatest rivers, the Nile and the Congo.

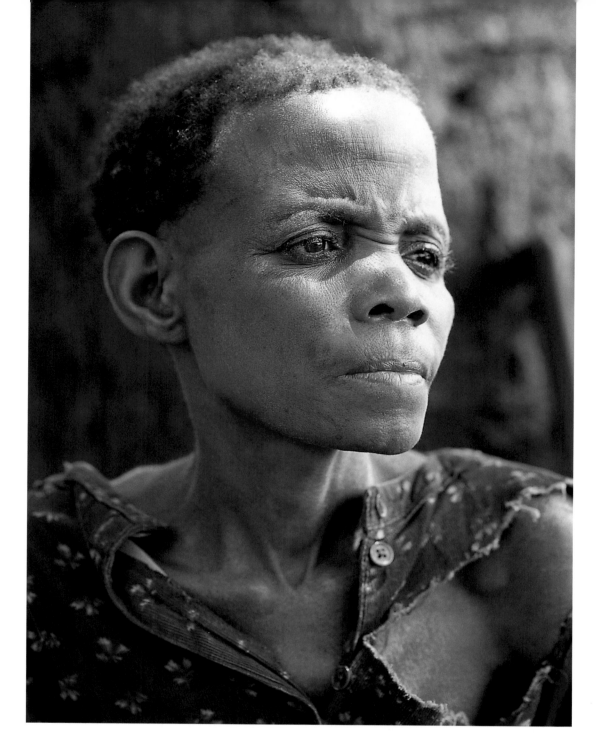

LEFT: Among the last hunter-gatherers to inhabit East Africa are the Bambuti, or Pygmies, of the Semliki Valley in the northern Albertine Rift.
OVERLEAF: Mating lions isolate themselves from the rest of the pride and stay together for up to three days, copulating every 15 to 20 minutes.

remarkable 37 birds, among them the enigmatic Congo Bay Owl, which was collected in the Itombwe Mountains in 1952 and has yet to be seen again (though its presence is suspected in Nyungwe) and the African Green Broadbill. This broadbill is one of several endemics that represent an isolated relict of a migrant Asian stock superseded elsewhere by indigenous African genera. Mammal taxa endemic to the Albertine Rift include the golden monkey and Rwenzori colobus – the latter known to move in troops of up to 400 individuals in Nyungwe – and the Rwenzori dwarf otter-shrew, which belongs to a family of aquatic insectivores that flourished some 50 million years ago and is elsewhere represented only by the related tenrecs of Madagascar.

The flagship Albertine Rift endemic is undoubtedly the charismatic mountain gorilla, whose plight was brought to global attention by the work undertaken by Dian Fossey in Rwanda prior to her brutal murder in 1985. One of the world's rarest large mammals, the mountain gorilla is confined to the dwindling forested habitats on the slopes of the six inactive Virunga volcanoes, where an estimated 350 to 400 individuals survive, while a second population of roughly 300 gorillas – according to recent DNA testing, probably racially distinct – inhabits Bwindi National Park.

Queen Elizabeth National Park

The Albertine Rift's rich mosaic of savanna, forest and wetlands converge on Uganda's Queen Elizabeth National Park (QENP), an area of tremendous biodiversity. This is attested to by a bird checklist of 610 species – the most varied birdlife of any African reserve, concentrated within an area less than one-tenth of the size of Kruger, Selous or Kafue.

No other conservation area comes quite so close to encapsulating the diversity of East Africa. The wetlands include lakes Edward and George, the steep-sided hippo-infested Kazinga Channel that connects them, a dense papyrus swamp listed as Uganda's only Ramsar Site, several forest-fringed rivers, and at least a dozen freshwater and saline crater lakes dating from an intense period of tectonic activity about 10 000 years ago. Terrestrial habitats include open grassland, euphorbia-studded savanna, well-developed acacia woodland, closed-canopy riparian woodland and lush tropical rainforest. As if that weren't enough, a skyward glance on a clear day will reveal the snow-capped Rwenzori peaks looming tall on the north-western skyline.

In common with Uganda's other savanna reserves, QENP lost much of its wildlife to war and poaching in the 1980s, with the elephant population, for instance, estimated to have declined from 4 000 to perhaps 150. However, 15 years on, the recovery, if not complete, is certainly well advanced. Elephant – now thought to number 1 200 – are abundant along the Kazinga Channel, which also hosts impressive numbers of buffalo and hippo, and is increasingly reliable for leopard and giant forest hog. Chimpanzees are resident in the forested Chambura Gorge; a wide variety of rare birds and monkeys inhabit the gorgeous Maramagambo Forest; lions are common on the Kasenyi Plains (as well as in the remote Ishasha Sector, where they regularly climb trees); while swampy areas support the iconic Shoebill and other papyrus specialists.

ABOVE: Bats are seldom seen by day, when they roost in trees or caves.
BELOW: An olive baboon in Queen Elizabeth National Park.
OPPOSITE ABOVE: More than 100 crater lakes dot the Rift Valley floor.
OPPOSITE BELOW: The Rwenzori Mountains rise to an altitude of 5 109 metres.

In addition to gorillas, the Albertine Rift is an important population centre for chimpanzees, and much of what we know about these humanlike apes derives from two long-standing behavioural research projects in the pair of Tanzanian national parks on Lake Tanganyika. These are the tiny Gombe Stream, where, in 1960, Jane Goodall initiated what is now the world's longest-running study of an individual wild animal population, and the much larger Mahale Mountains, where primatologists from Japan's University of Kyoto have studied a population of around 1 000 chimps since 1965.

With its crystal clear water and deserted sandy beaches hemmed by a sumptuous green escarpment, Lake Tanganyika is arguably the most beautiful of all the Rift Valley lakes. It is also the world's longest freshwater body, following the southern contours of the Albertine Rift for a full 675 kilometres, as well as the second deepest, holding a volume of water seven times greater than that of Lake Victoria. The lake hinterland is not quite so remote today as it was in 1871, when Stanley uttered the immortal words 'Doctor Livingstone, I presume?' at the small port of Ujiji. But it remains a thrillingly untrammelled part of East Africa, boasting few towns of any real substance, a quite appalling road network, and one of the continent's truly great public transport rides in the form of the MV *Liemba*, a German-built steamer that has been plying its length for almost a century!

OPPOSITE: Despite their imposing size and appearance, mountain gorillas are vegetarians.
ABOVE: Gorillas live in small, peaceable and predominantly terrestrial family groups of between five and fifty individuals in the mountains of the Albertine Rift.

Chimpanzees

Deep in the forest, an excited whoop erupts. This first solitary cry is immediately boosted by a dozen or more voices to become an overlapping chorus, which rises in volume, tempo and pitch to a frenzied shrieking crescendo. It winds down as abruptly as it began, leaving in its wake an aural vacuum. Jane Goodall called it the 'pant-hoot' call, a bonding ritual that allows chimpanzees within earshot to identify each other through their unique calls – and announces to the human intruder that contact with man's closest genetic relative is imminent.

Humans, chimpanzees and bonobos (pygmy chimpanzees) share roughly 98 per cent of their genetic code, making them more closely related to each other than to any other living creature, even gorillas. These similarities can be observed not only in the skeletal structure and skull, but also in the nervous and immune systems, and in many behavioural aspects. Bonobos, for instance, are the only primates other than humans to copulate in the missionary position.

Chimpanzees live in extended communities that forage in small, socially mobile subgroups which are centred around a few close family members. Male chimpanzees seldom leave the community into which they were born, whereas post-adolescent females regularly migrate into neighbouring communities. Every community has an alpha male, whose role is evidently quite benevolent – chairman of the board rather than crusty tyrant. He has the support of the other males of the group, except when a rival consciously contests his position.

Research projects initiated in the 1960s at Tanzania's Gombe Stream and Mahale Mountain national parks have revealed several behavioural differences best described as cultural. The palm-nut, though common to both reserves, is considered a delicacy by the Gombe chimps, but goes uneaten by their Mahale counterparts. Likewise, the 'termite-fishing' recorded at Gombe Stream has not ever been observed at Mahale, whose chimps often 'fish' arboreally for carpenter ants, behaviour that goes unrecorded at Gombe. More than any structural similarity, it is these cultural differences – the influence of nurture over nature – that underline our close genetic kinship with chimpanzees.

The genetic proximity of chimpanzees to humans is reflected in the strong individuality of their facial features and wide range of clearly distinguishable expressions, which include aggression (ABOVE), amiable curiosity (BELOW) and affection (OPPOSITE).

LAKE VICTORIA AND THE VICTORIA NILE

The people of Buganda, the ancient kingdom set at the heart of modern Uganda, know it as 'Nalubaale' – 'Home of the Spirits' – in reference to the powerful deities who they believe reside on its innumerable islands. The Arab slavers referred to it as 'Ukerewe' – still the name of its largest island – while the British explorer John Hanning Speke, the first European to stand on its shores, renamed it in honour of his queen. But whatever you choose to call it, Lake Victoria – shared between Tanzania, Uganda and Kenya – is the world's second-largest freshwater body, extending for 70 000 square kilometres across an elevated, shallow basin that separates the Gregory and Albertine rifts.

Lake Victoria has been subject to wide fluctuations in extent throughout its history. It took its present form as a result of an abrupt reversal in local drainage patterns caused by Rift-related tectonic activity some 12 000 years ago, immediately prior to which it had dried up entirely. The 200 cichlid species endemic to the lake have all evolved from a handful of common ancestors during that short period, the most recent such explosion of radial speciation anywhere on the planet. Ironically, these adaptable fish are today undergoing what one biologist has described as 'the greatest vertebrate mass extinction in recorded history', induced by the misconceived colonial-era introduction of the predatory Nile perch (which now constitutes 80 per cent of the lake's fish biomass) and a five-fold increase in algae levels and comparable drop in oxygenation caused by chemical pollution since the early twentieth century.

Local fluctuations in rainfall patterns are reflected in a dramatic contrast between the somewhat austere eastern lakeshore – open plains studded with granite koppies – and the altogether more lush fringing vegetation of tropical jungle to the north and west. Although it practically borders the Serengeti National Park, Lake Victoria has generally received little attention from conservation authorities, partially because it forms such an important centre of human settlement – an estimated 20 to 30 million people subsist in the lake basin, which supports four of East Africa's largest cities, namely Kampala, Mwanza, Kisumu and Jinja.

OPPOSITE: The largest protected area along the Victoria Nile is Murchison Falls National Park, whose elephant population has now recovered greatly from the heavy poaching of the 1970s and 1980s. ABOVE: The Nile crocodile, though capable of dragging terrestrial animals as large as wildebeest underwater, feeds mainly on fish in most parts of its range.

The most significant protected area on the lake, Tanzania's densely forested Rubondo Island National Park was gazetted in 1966 for development as a 'floating zoo' to breed endangered western rainforest species such as okapi and bongo. This plan was aborted in 1973, but not before small numbers of chimpanzee and black-and-white colobus were introduced, along with savanna animals such as elephant and giraffe (all still present today) and – less successfully – roan antelope and black rhinoceros. Of greater ecological significance than these introduced mammals is the island's uniquely dense population of the semi-aquatic sitatunga antelope, and the wealth of birds that occur naturally in its forested interior and swampy bays.

Speke's arrival at the lakeshore, near present-day Mwanza in 1858, fuelled one of the fiercest geographical debates of the Victorian era. Speke was convinced that this vast inland sea was the source of the White Nile; his former travelling companion, Sir Richard Burton, was equally certain that the great river flowed out of Lake Tanganyika, which the two men had reached together a year previously. In 1863, Speke returned to Lake Victoria and reached the site of present-day Jinja, where a substantial river exited the lake over a waterfall reckoned by Speke to be 'by far the most interesting sight I had seen in Africa'. However, neither Speke's proclamation that 'The Nile is settled', nor his accidental death by a self-inflicted gun wound in 1864, did anything to ease the debate, which was settled only in 1877 after Henry Stanley spent three years methodically testing the three contemporaneous theories regarding the Nile's source, and concluded that Speke had been correct.

BELOW: Lake Victoria and the Nile support a prodigious variety of water-associated birds, such as the ornamentally marked Pygmy Goose, an uncommon resident of lily-covered pools, and (OPPOSITE) the Yellow-billed Stork, which normally feeds in the shallows of large rivers and lakes.

A land that time forgot

THE ABYSSINIAN HIGHLANDS

Ethiopia has been described as 'the Tibet of Africa' – a devout, isolated and ruggedly individualistic montane empire, steeped in myth and legend, routinely misrepresented by the mass media, and, above all, impenetrably and wonderfully strange. Contrary to popular perception, Ethiopia is dominated not by deserts, but by the Abyssinian Highlands, an elevated plateau of grassy meadows and wild, lofty peaks that covers an area larger than Great Britain and forms the watershed for the mighty Blue Nile as well as three lesser river systems.

As majestically beautiful as they are agriculturally bountiful, the extensive, fertile Abyssinian Highlands are isolated on all sides by low-lying, arid country. Because of this, they bear many of the hallmarks of an island ecology, in particular a long list of endemics – species found nowhere else in the world – that includes five large mammals, 30 birds and innumerable smaller vertebrates, invertebrates and plants.

'The most marvellous of all Abyssinian landscapes,' according to the Edwardian traveller Rosita Forbes, are the Simien Mountains, which lie to the north of Lake Tana, the main source of the Blue Nile. Forbes's evocative description continues: 'Ancient hills, now eroded into hundreds of pinnacles and buttresses opened before us, as we looked across a gorge of clouded amethyst ... A thousand years ago, when the old gods reigned in Ethiopia, they must have played chess with these stupendous crags.'

OPPOSITE: Giant lobelias and chilly tarns adorn the 4 000-metre-high Sanetti Plateau, which supports the world's largest tract of Afro-Alpine moorland.
BELOW: Tis Abay, or 'Smoke of the Nile', is one of Africa's most impressive waterfalls.

147

The Ethiopian wolf

Sometimes also referred to as the red jackal or Simien fox, the Ethiopian wolf *Canis simensis* shares stronger genetic affinities with the Eurasian wolf than any other living African canine, a clear example of how Ethiopia's fauna and flora contain elements typical of both the Afro-tropical and Palaearctic zones.

A highly specialized diurnal feeder, the Ethiopian wolf is a courser that feeds opportunistically on a diet of giant mole rats and other rodents that thrive in the moorland and short grassland of Ethiopia's higher mountains. Formerly widespread in such habitats, the Ethiopian wolf has suffered a dramatic slide in numbers over recent decades. Habitat loss and hunting have played a part in this decline, but the primary cause has been epidemics of exotic canine diseases carried by domestic dogs, which, for instance, wiped out most of the Simien Mountains' population in the 1960s, and reduced the population of the Web Valley (one of three main wolf habitats in Bale National Park) by 80 per cent in 2003.

Listed by the World Conservation Union (IUCN) as critically endangered, the Ethiopian wolf is the world's most rare canid and Africa's most immediately threatened predator. Current estimates place the total population of this Ethiopian endemic at 450 individuals, and roughly half of these animals are concentrated in the Bale Mountains. The remainder are scattered across six other sites countrywide. Particularly during the rainy season, packs of up to 15 of these alert and confiding creatures – their warm rufous coats broken up by bold white throat and flank markings – might congregate around one den. It is sobering to think that a group like this represents about 7 per cent of the Bale population and more than 3 per cent of the global one.

*A signpost (**ABOVE**) warns motorists to be on the alert for the critically endangered Ethiopian wolf (**BELOW AND OPPOSITE**), which lives in small family packs.*

ABOVE: Mules are put to use as pack animals in the Simien Mountains of northern Ethiopia, whose 4 620-metre-high Ras Dashen is the fourth-highest peak in Africa.

The Simien Mountains consist of a rugged, undulating plateau, incised by steep, narrow gorges and bounded on three sides by a massive escarpment that drops a sheer kilometre in places. The range reaches an elevation of 4 620 metres at Ras Dashen, the fourth-highest peak in Africa, and it supports a typical Afro-montane vegetation cover of grass, moss and heather, studded with tall, otherworldly giant lobelias.

Protected within the Simien Mountains National Park, parts of the range are accessible by road, but it is essentially the domain of trekkers, who normally explore it over a few days by mule. Although the main attraction of the high Simiens is undoubtedly the scenery, the range is a stronghold for several endemic or endangered species, including the northern race of Ethiopian wolf, the very rare *Walia ibex*, and the magnificent Lammergeyer, or bearded vulture.

The most common large mammal in the Simiens, however, is the gelada *Thercopithecus gelada*, a striking and unmistakable primate endemic to Ethiopia. The male gelada is a spectacularly handsome beast, with an imposing golden mane and heart-shaped red chest patch – the latter thought to serve the same purpose as the colourful buttocks or testicles found on other African monkeys. Something of a living fossil, the gelada is the sole surviving representative of a formerly wide-ranging monkey genus that feeds exclusively on grass and is ancestral to the modern baboon (which has displaced it in savanna habitats) as well as to the terrestrial drills and arboreal mangabeys of the western rainforests.

The gelada is the most sociable of African monkeys, with conglomerations of 500 or more regularly recorded grazing in one field. The harem-based social structure of a gelada troop is regarded as the most complex of any animal other than humans, and males within any given troop regularly fight with each other to assert their dominance and their associated mating privileges. A gelada troop spends its entire day grazing on the high plateau, before retiring to the safe shelter of the cliffs for the night.

In contrast to the austere grandeur of the Simiens, the Bale Mountains in the southeast – also protected within a national park – comprise pretty rolling green slopes covered in lush grassland and fragrant juniper-hagenia forest. The park headquarters at Dinsho form an important sanctuary for endemic forest birds such as the Abyssinian Catbird. They are also home to the handsome mountain nyala, which was the last African antelope to be described by European zoologists. First collected in 1908, this large spiral-horned antelope – endemic to Ethiopia – is misleadingly named, since it is closer in size and appearance to the greater kudu than to the nyala of southern Africa.

A quiet country road leads southeast from Dinsho to the small highland towns of Robe and Goba, where the local Oromo people, draped in characteristic blankets, are often seen riding to market or herding their prized cattle. Past Goba, the road ascends through slopes dotted with red hot poker aloes to the flat open moorland of the 4 000-metre-high Sanetti Plateau. Bracing climate and thin air aside, this is a fantastic landscape, with a pastel cover of grey and white mosses and heather interspersed with stands of giant lobelias and small blue tarns. The last major stronghold of the Ethiopian wolf, the rarest of all African predators, the Sanetti Plateau is also an excellent place to see a number of bird species endemic to Ethiopia, such as the Spot-throated Lapwing, the Blue-winged Goose and the peculiar Rouget's Rail.

BELOW: A giant lobelia protrudes from the pastel-hued heather tussocks of the 4 000-metre-high Sanetti Plateau, which supports the largest contiguous area of Afro-Alpine moorland on the continent.

RIGHT: Resembling a shaggier version of the more widespread greater kudu, the mountain nyala is an endangered Ethiopian endemic whose global population of 4 000 is concentrated on the Bale Mountains and adjacent Arsi Highlands in southern Ethiopia.

BELOW AND OPPOSITE: The magnificent gelada is unique among African primates in being a herd grazer – an ecological niche which is filled elsewhere by bovines and other ungulates.

The origin of man

'It is somewhat more probable,' suggested Charles Darwin in his creationist-baiting 1871 publication *The Descent of Man*, 'that our early progenitors lived on the African continent than elsewhere'. More than a century later, a mass of fossil evidence supports Darwin's once-scandalous proposition, and, while the specifics of human evolution remain controversial, practically every one of the dozen-or-so extinct hominid species recognized by modern palaeontologists was first discovered in the vicinity of the East African Rift.

The most famous site is Tanzania's Olduvai Gorge, where a 1,75 million-year-old jawbone discovered in 1959 provided the first conclusive support for Darwin's 'Out Of Africa' hypothesis, while also pushing the timescale of human evolution past the million-year mark. Another key site is Hadar, in Ethiopia, which leapt to prominence in 1974 following the discovery of the skull of a female hominid – nicknamed Lucy after the Beatles' song popular at the time – who lived almost four million years earlier.

The timescale over which humans have inhabited the Rift Valley is unimaginably vast, and recent years have seen a spate of exciting new finds. In Ethiopia several 5,8 million-year-old fossils of forest-dwelling hominids have been discovered since 1997. This has undermined the established theory that bipedalism evolved in a savanna habitat. In Kenya, meanwhile, two different fossils described in 2001 and placed in new genera have been cited as progenitors of the genus *Homo* (which includes modern man), supporting a hypothesis that the *Australopithecus* line represented by the Olduvai and Hadar fossils constitutes an evolutionary 'dead end'.

The Rift Valley is often alluded to as the Cradle of Mankind, and it's certainly possible that some or all of the pivotal steps in human evolution actually did occur there, though the main reason why palaeontologists have worked the Rift so heavily is that it possesses a wealth of sites suited to fossil recovery. Ironically, the world's oldest-known hominid fossil is a 6,5-million-year-old skull discovered in 2001 in Chad, thousands of kilometres to the northwest. The jury is out on whether this isolated, skeleton-less skull represents a proto-human, a proto-chimpanzee, a proto-gorilla – or something else entirely. However, it certainly highlights the element of 'seek-and-ye-shall-find' that informs the notion of the Rift as the fulcrum of human evolution.

Situated in a semi-arid part of Maasailand on the border of the Serengeti National Park and the Ngorongoro Conservation Area, Olduvai Gorge (OPPOSITE) is an important hominid site, originally worked by Louis and Mary Leakey, who uncovered a 1.75 million-year-old jawbone of Australopithecus boisei there in 1959. A replica of this skull is displayed in the site museum (BELOW LEFT), along with the fossilized skulls of several extinct animals (BELOW CENTRE) and a selection of Stone Age tools (BELOW RIGHT) that were found at Olduvai Gorge.

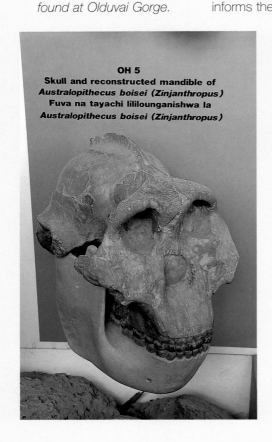

Whispers and legends

HIGHLAND CULTURE

Just as the ecology of the Abyssinian Highlands has been moulded by its isolation from similar habitats, so too has its cultural and historical development been shaped by sporadic bursts of contact with the outside world, interspersed with far longer periods of isolation and introspection. Ethiopia has been a rich source of legend since Old Testament times, when it is said that the illegitimate son of King Solomon and the Queen of Sheba travelled to Ethiopia to found the ancient city of Axum. By the time of Christ, this city ruled over a trade empire regarded contemporaneously as one of the three most powerful in the world.

Influenced by the Egyptian Coptic Church, the rulers of Axum converted to Christianity in the fourth century AD. Four centuries later, the rise of Islam in neighbouring parts of Arabia caused Axum to decline as a trading power, and to be cut off from other Christian denominations. So it was that the Ethiopian Orthodox Church evolved in isolation from other denominations as, in the words of Gibbon, 'the Ethiopians slept for close on a thousand years, forgetful of the world, by which they were forgotten'.

Centuries later, rumours of the so-called Kingdom of Prester John – an isolated Christian empire deep in the heart of Africa – reached mediaeval Europe. In the sixteenth century, after the Portuguese sailed around the tip of Africa, they arrived at that legendary kingdom to encounter an almost unrecognizable faith – unambiguously Christian, but imbued with ancient Judaic customs such as male circumcision and dancing in the aisles, which had long before been discarded or deemed heretical by Rome. Even today, anybody who has witnessed an Ethiopian mass – sombre, white-robed priests swaying to interminable, atonal Arabic chants – will feel that they have been transported through time to a ceremony not dissimilar to Christianity as it must have been practised by the earliest converts.

The air of anachronistic stoicism that characterizes Ethiopian Christianity finds its most haunting outward expression in the 300 or more churches carved by hand into the solid rock faces of the Abyssinian Highlands. The most architecturally inspired of these edifices is the subterranean complex of churches, chapels, courtyards and alleys that were carved into the hillside of Lalibela during the thirteenth century. Often cited as the Eighth Wonder of the Ancient World, the churches of Lalibela were visited in 1521 by the Portuguese priest Francisco Alvares, whose awed but sketchy description concluded: 'It wearied me to write more of these works, because it seemed to me they would accuse me of untruth.'

One can empathize with Alvares. Even today, Lalibela defies belief – a labyrinthine complex of 12 subterranean churches and chapels, ringed by trenches and connected by numerous tunnels and passageways, hand-carved from the rock chip by painstaking chipping. Bet Medhane Alem, 11,5 metres high and with a floor area of 800 square metres, is the largest rock-hewn edifice in the world. More impressive still is Bet Giorgis, a cruciform monolith 15 metres high and enclosed by a trench just as tall. But what makes Lalibela so special is that, far from being a museum piece left behind by a vanished civilization, it is a slice of living history, still in active use, and populated by a somewhat Biblical cast of robed villagers, studious hermits, chanting priests and muttering nuns. These churches remain, as they have been for 800 years, the spiritual focus of a remote Christian community set high in the chilly mountains of Ethiopia.

OPPOSITE: The royal compound in the city of Gonder contains several seventeenth-century castles built by a succession of Ethiopian kings with the assistance of Portuguese and Indian masons.
ABOVE: The annual ceremony of Meskel, a uniquely Ethiopian Christian tradition commemorating the discovery of the True Cross, takes place every September in the ancient Ethiopian capital of Axum.

157

OPPOSITE: White-robed worshippers in the brilliantly painted church of Debre Birhan Selassie. LEFT: An incense-carrying priest exits the side door of one of the rock-hewn churches of Lalibela. OVERLEAF: An Afar camel caravan carries salt blocks mined in the Danakil Desert to the highland town of Mekele in the northernmost Ethiopian province of Tigray.

TOP: A priest reads from an illuminated Bible, one of numerous mediaeval treasures which are hoarded away in Ethiopia's rock-hewn churches.
ABOVE: Worshippers enjoy a post-mass drink of *t'ella*, or millet beer, at a holy day outside the remote monastery of Abba Yohanni.

North of Lalibela, at least 120 churches are carved into the remote sandstone crags of the province of Tigray, three-quarters of them still in active use. Incredibly, the existence of the vast majority of these magnificent excavations was unsuspected by other Ethiopians, let alone foreigners, prior to the 1960s. Even today, the churches might go months, even years, between receiving foreign visitors, and they retain an aura of serenity and devotion borne of this deep isolation.

Ease of access was clearly not a priority when the churches were excavated, and many must be reached by ascending a staggeringly steep footpath. Most dramatic of all is the small chapel of Abuna Yemata Guh, which, aside from its elaborate interior of fifteenth-century paintings, is remarkable for being situated at the pinnacle of a 200-metre sandstone pillar and only accessible via a sheer face pockmarked with handholds worn smooth over centuries of use. Other Tigrayan churches, though not as difficult to access, are so well disguised that they cannot be seen until one is just metres from the entrance – a fine example being Maryam Hibito, which aptly translates as 'the Hidden Mary'!

The church of Abuna Abraham Debre Tsion, regarded by church expert Ruth Plant as 'one of the great churches of the Tigray, both from the architectural and devotional aspect', is named after the sixth-century saint who was reputedly responsible for its excavation and now lies buried beneath it.

The rock-hewn churches of Ethiopia rank as among the most atmospheric active religious shrines anywhere in the world. But this ancient country boasts a great many other archaeological gems, ranging from the celebrated field of monolithic granite stelae that stand up to 33 metres tall on the outskirts of Axum itself and a well-preserved 2 600-year-old pre-Christian temple at Yeha, to the monastic islands of Lake Tana and the cluster of seventeenth-century castles in the nearby city of Gondar.

Above all, however, the fascination of this determinedly eccentric land rests on what the noted travel writer Dervla Murphy referred to as an 'Orlando-like illusion of travelling through different centuries' – an atmosphere that makes continuous and bemusing shifts between the Biblical, the mediaeval, and the unabashedly modern.

ABOVE: The church of Bet Gebriel-Rafael in Lalibela is reached via a rickety wooden bridge across a 5-metre-deep dry moat.

Valley of nomads

WITHIN THE GREGORY RIFT

Storm clouds gather over the ragged volcanic peaks that punctuate the monotone acacia scrub of the Maasai Steppes. Elephants in a herd emerge from the long shadow cast by the 900-metre-high burnished cliffs of the Rift Valley escarpment, and thendawdle across the flood plain to the water's edge, to scatter an assembly of Yellow-billed Storks and scolding plovers. Flocks of queleas streak through the sky, while pelicans bob ponderously across the lake whose setting Hemingway once described as 'the loveliest I had seen in Africa'.

Lake Manyara, which has given its name to a national park famed for mighty tuskers and quirky, tree-climbing lions, has been described as a 'vast puddle'. It extends for 40 kilometres at the foot of the Rift escarpment, yet, on average, is less than a metre deep. Drained solely by evaporation, Manyara's water is saturated with mineral deposits and prone to marked fluctuations in extent – features it shares with several of the 30-odd lakes that stud the floor of the Gregory Rift between central Tanzania and northern Ethiopia.

Probably the most renowned of these lakes is Nakuru, where, in ideal conditions, up to 1,5 million flamingos gather in the shallows to feed on the algae that proliferate in its shallow, alkaline water. It's a compelling spectacle, as a flock of several hundred birds might rise above the general squawk-and-chatter to reveal a harmony of pink-and-black underwings. The full scale of the phenomenon is apparent from the surrounding cliffs, where the individual birds blend into a solid, shimmering pink band that separates the green water from its bleached, soda-encrusted rim.

Nakuru means 'Place of Waterbuck' in the local dialect. As the centrepiece of the only Kenyan national park to be fully fenced, it's also an important relocation site for endangered animals such as black and white rhino – there's no better place to see either species in Kenya – and Rothschild's giraffe. And when the flamingos aren't present, they're most likely to be settled at nearby Lake Bogoria. Bogoria is a soda lake fed by explosive hot springs, which – like Manyara – lies below a spectacular stretch of craggy Rift escarpment.

OPPOSITE: Barabaig girls dance at the funeral of an important village elder, whose corpse is interred in a seated position in the circular mud-and-stick *bung'eda* behind them.
BELOW: The string of Rift Valley lakes running through Ethiopia, Kenya and Tanzania attracts prodigious flocks of water-associated birds such as Great White Pelicans, seen here at Lake Nakuru.
OVERLEAF: Aggregations of up to one million Lesser Flamingos are regularly present on Lake Bogoria.

165

Samburu wildlife

Something of an 'Africa through the looking glass' quality pervades Samburu, Buffalo Springs and Shaba, the trio of semi-contiguous reserves that flank the Ewaso Nyiro River as it cuts through the austere badlands dividing Kenya's central highlands from Ethiopia. There is, for a start, something profoundly incongruous about the very presence of a substantial waterway in this landscape of rocky plains studded with bare termite mounds and thorny acacia scrub. Furthermore, a luxuriant ribbon of riparian woodland supporting the like of waterbuck and vervet monkey flanks this river.

Odder still is some of the dry-country wildlife that inhabits these scrubby plains. The endangered and highly localized Grevy's zebra, for instance, is almost twice as bulky as the familiar Burchell's zebra, and more handsome too, with its dense narrow stripes tapering to a fine circular pattern on the rump. No less of an anomaly is the reticulated giraffe, distinguished by its neat geometrically-marked coat, and – like Grevy's zebra – now more-or-less endemic to northern Kenya as a result of poaching elsewhere in its limited range.

Samburu is home to many dry-country antelope including the regal Beisa oryx, the secretive lesser kudu, and unusual long-horned races of Grant's gazelle and impala. Then there's the gerenuk. As its Swahili name *swala twiga* (antelope giraffe) suggests, an extraordinarily distended neck and freakishly small head distinguish it. These features allow it to feed by stretching almost erect on its hind legs to nibble on the leaves that most other browsers can't reach.

The unusual fauna of Samburu also embraces a substantial number of birds endemic to the arid Somali biome of northeast Africa. These include the Somali Bee-eater, Somali Ostrich, Golden-breasted Starling and – most spectacular of all – the Vulturine Guineafowl, whose brilliant cobalt chest contrasts strikingly with its flowing white neck feathers.

*Dry-country 'specials' associated with Samburu National Reserve include the brilliantly coloured Vulterine Guineafowl (**ABOVE**), the long-necked gerenuk (**BELOW**) and the narrow-striped Grevy's zebra (**OPPOSITE**).*

Facial and body decoration

Nothing else in Ethiopia prepares one for South Omo. Nor, for that matter, does much else in modern Africa. Entering the remote badlands that flank the Omo River feels like a journey not merely through space, but through time, into the midst of a miscellany of defiantly traditionalist pastoralists who inhabit a physical and psychic landscape little different to that of their nomadic ancestors.

In South Omo, the African propensity for bodily decoration and scarification is taken to extremes. Take the Hamer, the most populous of the region's tribes, whose women wear a heavy fringe of thick ochre plaits, leather skirts decorated with cowries, a dozen or more copper bracelets and a thick copper necklace. Both sexes adorn their bodies with permanent welts created by cutting the skin open with a razor and then treating the resultant wound with ash.

By contrast, the Karo – who number fewer than 1 000 individuals – are known for the body painting the men indulge in before important ceremonies. They dab their torsos with white chalk paint in imitation of guineafowl plumage, and prepare colourful facemasks with chalk, charcoal, powdered yellow rock and iron ore pastes. The hairstyle favoured by Karo women is also rather striking: tightly cropped at the side, tied into bulbous knots and dyed ochre, it looks rather like a garish orange shower cap.

All of which is rather mundane by comparison with the Mursi and their lip-plates. Customarily, when a Mursi woman reaches her late teens, a slit is cut below her lower lip. Over the next year, the gap is progressively stretched until a small circular clay plate, indented like a pulley, can be inserted. As the lip stretches further, so the plate is replaced with a larger one, a process that's repeated until eventually a clay plate of perhaps 15 centimetres in diameter can be inserted. The larger the lip-plate she can wear, the greater the woman's bride value – should she be able to pull her distended lower lip over and behind her head, she might fetch 50 head of cattle.

CLOCKWISE FROM ABOVE:

Hamer boy with mono-chrome facial painting; Karo elders indulge in mutual body painting; Hamer woman with ochre-dyed plaited hair; Hamer man with clay hair bun; Mursi woman with lip-plate.

TOP: A Maasai warrior.
ABOVE: A black robe
and white fringe are
traditionally worn by
teenage Maasai girls for
a few weeks after they
have undergone the widely
practised ritual known as
'female circumcision'.

With the exception of the lakes and their immediate hinterland, the dry Gregory Rift is better suited to a nomadic lifestyle than to cultivation and permanent settlement. Even today, the region remains almost continuously inhabited by semi-nomadic pastoralists. Among them are the iconic Maasai, whose dedication to the ancient cattle-rearing lifestyle – and stubborn adherence to an animist religion and such officially frowned-upon practices as polygamy, ritual circumcision and female genital mutilation – remains quite remarkable. But the Maasai are not alone in their refusal to submit to cultural homogenization. There are also the closely related Samburu of the semi-desert country to the north of Mount Kenya, the Barabaig of the central Tanzanian Rift, and the Borena of southern Ethiopia – to name but a few of the distinct tribal groupings whose traditional attire adds a splash of colour to the dusty dry Rift Valley floor.

East Africa's pastoralists typically measure a man's wealth in terms of cattle (or, in more arid areas, camels) and children. A herd of 50 cattle would qualify as respectable, and the more children the better. A man who has plenty of one, but few of the other is still poor. Most pastoralists feed almost exclusively off their livestock, and regard it as beneath their dignity to hunt, to eat vegetable matter or to fish. Because cows are more valuable alive than dead, they are generally slaughtered on special occasions only. The everyday pastoralist diet typically consists of cow's milk, or the meat of smaller livestock such as goats or, in the case of the Maasai, a cocktail of fermented milk blended with blood drained from a strategic nick in the jugular vein of a cow.

The cultural insularity of the Rift Valley pastoralists reaches surreal heights in the harsh badlands that slope towards Lake Turkana. This 200-kilometre-long sump, also known as the Jade Sea, glistens jewel-like amid the bleak volcanic rockscapes of northern Kenya. This is the 'half of Kenya about which the other half knows nothing and cares even less', in the words of pre-World War II traveller Negley Farson. It was the last part of East Africa to be explored by outsiders – Turkana was no more than a rumour prior to the Von Teliki expedition of 1888 – while the last of the region's cartographic blanks was filled as recently as 1909.

A century later, when confronted by the vast arid expanses of northern Kenya, by the Samburu, Gabbra, Turkana and Rendille herdsmen who trail along its rocky earth, it doesn't take an overwrought imagination to sense something of Africa as it must have been before the intrusion of slave traders, missionaries and colonists. Yet the notion of northern Kenya as 'Africa unchanged' is in many senses an illusion. Traditionally, this is the domain of true nomads, people whose endless struggle to subsist in a merciless environment has been mirrored by a perpetual state of motion and territorial conflict. Ironically, it was the colonists who entrenched the modern tribal boundaries of northern Kenya, freezing once fluid boundaries as they happened to stand in the early years of the twentieth century ... and as line after arbitrary line was drawn across the formerly uncharted desert, life for the nomads could never be quite the same.

Another arbitrarily imposed border divides northern Kenya from the Ethiopian region of South Omo, named for the Omo River, which rises in the highlands around Addis Ababa and empties into the remote northern tip of Lake Turkana. Here, some 30-odd agro-pastoralist tribes – many numbering no more than a few hundred individuals – collectively represent four of Africa's major linguistic groups, one of which is unique to this small area. Largely untouched by (and uninterested in) exotic influences, the people of South Omo seem intent on outdoing each other when it comes to such rituals and decorations as torso scarification, lip-plates, lip-plugs, body painting, bull-jumping, totem worship and stick fighting. Certainly, it is easy enough to believe that as recently as 50 years ago, most of the residents of South Omo were unaware that Ethiopia existed.

Much of the southern Ethiopian Rift is occupied by a series of lakes whose scenic beauty – and spectacular birdlife – approximates that of their Kenyan counterparts. The far northeast of Ethiopia, by contrast, is the site of the most primal of all Rift landscapes. In this desolate and inaccessible place the smoke-belching Mount Erte Ale, whose crater holds the world's only permanent lake of molten lava, towers above the Dallol Depression. This long-extinct saltpan that dips to 116 metres below sea level is officially ranked the hottest place in the world!

This remote and inhospitable thirstland is home to nomadic Afar salt-miners whose caravans have supplied bars of coarse salt to the nearby Abyssinian Highlands since Biblical times. Recent decades have seen a trend towards urbanization among the Afar, but the nomadic lifestyle is widely practised and the ferocious Afro-haired appearance of the rural camel-herders has remained unchanged for centuries. As recently as the 1930s, it was customary for Afar men to kill any male intruder and lop off his testicles as a trophy. These days, however, their traditional 40-centimetre-long curved daggers (often supplemented with rifles) are more likely to be put to fatal use in disputes between rivals.

ABOVE: A Karo boy looks out over the remote and rugged Omo River before it empties into Lake Turkana on the Ethiopian border with Kenya.

173

Hunter-gatherers

The notion that the Rift Valley pastoralists represent one last fragile link with pre-agricultural human society is placed in sobering context by the realization that modern humans have inhabited the area for something like 500 000 years, yet domestic livestock were introduced in around 2000 BC. Put simply, for some 99 per cent of their tenure – 99,9 per cent if you include our earliest hominid ancestors – the people of the Rift were not herders at all, but exclusive hunter-gatherers.

The Hadza of northern Tanzania are possibly the last true savanna-dwelling adherents to the foraging lifestyle that served humankind so well for countless millennia. They live in semi-nomadic family bands, using rudimentary grass encampments as a base for anything up to one month before they move on. The Hadza are fairly indiscriminate about what they eat – anything from a mouse to a giraffe is considered fair game – but baboons are the ultimate delicacy, while roots, seeds, tubers and fruit account for about 80 per cent of their food intake.

Many Hadza still dress in the traditional attire of animal skins, and they refuse to be coerced into a more settled way of life. In the 1960s, the government built them a brick settlement with piped water, schools, clinics and access to good agricultural land. Within 10 years, the model village had been all but abandoned as the Hadza returned to their preferred hunter-gatherer lifestyle. The government has since accepted the Hadza's right to lead the life of their choice. A large tract of communal land fringing Lake Eyasi is set aside for their use and they remain the only Tanzanian tribe automatically exempt from tax payment!

The Hadza tongue belongs to the Khoisan linguistic family, which dominated eastern and southern Africa until perhaps 3 000 years ago, to be displaced as migrant Bantu-speaking agriculturists and pastoralists forced hunter-gatherers into territory unsuited to herding or cultivation. This process of marginalization has hastened over the past century: of the 100 Khoisan languages documented, only 30 are still spoken today, by fewer than 200 000 people continent-wide. That most Khoisan languages, if not already obsolete, are headed that way, takes on an added poignancy if, as some linguists believe, their unique click sounds are a preserved element of the very earliest language – a fading echo of the first human voices to have carried across the African plains.

ABOVE: A Kalahari bushman prepares for a moonlight hunt.
BELOW: Modern hunter-gatherers supplement their traditional tools with western artefacts, such as cups and cans.
OPPOSITE: The Hadza of northern Tanzania rely on dogs to help them track their quarries.

THE EASTERN ARC AND RIFT VALLEY MOUNTAINS

In 1848, Johan Rebmann, a German missionary based in the Taita Hills, heard rumours of a large silver-capped mountain inhabited by an evil spirit that froze to death anybody who tried to ascend it. Intrigued, Rebmann visited the base of the mountain, and immediately recognized its silvery peak for what it is. When his report of the discovery was published, however, the general reaction was open derision. It would be another 12 years before the existence of Kilimanjaro – and of the equatorial snow-cap that had so outraged European geographers – was confirmed by the respected geologist Von der Decken, and accorded widespread acceptance.

Almost 150 years later, Kilimanjaro is probably Africa's single most recognizable natural landmark, spending long days with its peak concealed in the clouds, before abruptly shedding its cover, usually at dusk or dawn, to reveal a sight that truly does need to be seen to be believed. It is not so much the absolute altitude of the peak that impresses – at 5 895 metres it is the highest point in Africa, but something of a dwarf by Himalayan standards. Rather, it is the fact that it rises in absolute isolation for 5 kilometres above the hot, dusty plains below that is so remarkable. Measured from base to peak, rather than relative to sea level, Kilimanjaro is quite simply the tallest freestanding mountain in the world.

The mountain ranges and isolated peaks that flank the Gregory Rift, or rise from the coastal belt to the east of the Rift, can be dated to one of three spates of geological activity. The most ancient of these occurred perhaps two billion years ago, when a collision between two tectonic plates created a quartzite mountain range comparable in scale to the modern Himalayas, the most substantial single relict of which is the Mbeya range in southern Tanzania. Somewhat more modern are the so-called Eastern Arc Mountains, a loose crescent of 13 isolated ranges, all but one set in present-day Tanzania. These formed about 100 million years ago, along a fault to the east of the modern-day Rift Valley.

Youthful in geological terms, Kilimanjaro is one of several volcanic mountains associated with the formation of the Gregory Rift, having first erupted about one million years ago and remained active until about 350 000 years ago. Of a similar volcanic origin are mounts Kenya, Meru and Elgon, respectively the second-, fifth- and ninth-highest mountains in Africa, all of which are older than Kilimanjaro and would have stood taller than it does today when they were still active. Most of the Rift-associated volcanoes are now extinct, or long dormant, but Mount Rungwe, which lies close to the juncture of the three main branches of the Rift, last erupted about 300 years ago, and a series of recent tremors suggest that it might be brewing up for renewed action. However, the Maasai's 'Mountain of God', Ol Doinyo L'Engai, is more active. Its steep slopes were denuded by four eruptions in the twentieth century, and its crater has been refilling with lava since 1996.

The mountains of East Africa possess something akin to an island ecology – indeed, the high levels of endemism associated with the Eastern Arc in particular have led to it being dubbed an 'African Galapagos'. This is a function of the antiquity of its rain-forests, which have flourished continuously over the past 30 million years, thanks to reliable gusts of airborne moisture from the Indian Ocean. Isolated from the central African lowland rainforest some 10 million years ago, the individual Eastern Arc ranges have subsequently become isolated from one another, transforming them – most especially the Usambara, Uluguru and Udzungwa ranges – into one of the world's top 20 biodiversity hotspots.

OPPOSITE: Mount Meru, Africa's fifth-highest mountain, as seen from the upper slopes of nearby Kilimanjaro.
BELOW: Tired hikers enjoy the view on a clear morning from the Roof of Africa – the 5 895-metre-high peak of Kilimanjaro.

At least 75 vertebrate species – including 10 birds and 10 mammals – are Eastern Arc endemics, with species such as Usambara Akalat, Loveridge's Sunbird and Uluguru Bush-Shrike restricted to one specific range. As for the flora, 2 850 species have been identified in the Usambara alone, a list that includes 680 different trees, a greater tally than for North America and Europe combined. Of 16 endemic plant genera, the most familiar is the genus *Saintpaulia* – the African violet, a popular perennial pot plant that generates a global trade worth tens of millions of US dollars, yet is endangered within its restricted natural range.

Eastern Arc endemics fall into two broad categories: old endemics that show little divergence from relict evolutionary lineages, and new endemics representing recently evolved lineages. A clear example of the former 'living fossil' category is the giant elephant-shrew, which is almost identical in structure to 20-million-year-old fossils. In some cases, these more stable endemics are affiliated to extant West African species from which they have become isolated – among the larger mammals, the two monkey species endemic to Udzungwa – the Uhehe red colobus and the Sanje crested mangabey, the latter unknown to science until 1979 – are cases in point.

The origins of new endemics are more variable. Some, such as African violets, evolved from ancestral stock blown across from Madagascar in a freak cyclone. Others, including many of the birds and flying insects, are essentially local variations on similar species found in the neighbouring savanna or in other forests. By contrast, the Udzungwa Partridge, an evolutionary relict discovered as recently as 1991, has stronger genetic affiliations to the Asian hill partridges than to any African bird, suggesting that it colonized the area at a time when a forested passage linked Africa and Asia via the Arabian peninsula.

BELOW: A young cowherd rests outside a Wa-Arusha hut on the verdant foot-slopes of Mount Meru.

On taller mountains, such as Kilimanjaro and Kenya, the forest gives way at about 3 000 metres to an otherworldly Afro-Alpine zone of clumped multi-hued heath, studded by desolate stands of giant lobelia and groundsel. Unlike the forest, this bleak, chilly ecosystem supports low levels of diversity – fewer than 60 plant species are known from above the 4 000-metre contour of Kilimanjaro, for instance – though a couple of bird species, including the Hill Chat and Scarlet-tufted Malachite Sunbird, are endemic to this rarefied montane habitat.

ABOVE: Elephants march across a clearing in the lush forest zone of Mount Kenya, the second-highest mountain in Africa.

Ngorongoro Crater

A thin mist swirls through an enchanted forest of gnarled, lichen-draped trees. Several hundred metres below, fully encircled by mountains, a hazy expanse of almost treeless savanna dips towards an oval soda lake. The lake shimmers pink as the first rays of sun refract off innumerable flamingos, flocked along its edges. As the mist dissipates further, a distant ant-like formation inches across the grassy plain: a herd of hundreds upon hundreds of wildebeest and zebra are setting off. Another day is breaking over Africa's most spectacular natural arena: the Ngorongoro Crater.

The relict of an extinct volcano that once stood taller than Kilimanjaro does today, Ngorongoro is the largest intact caldera in the world, and the view from its forested rim – sheer walls dropping 600 metres to enclose a 260-square-kilometre expanse of fertile savanna – defies superlatives. With every change in the sky the majesty of the crater is revealed – it is milky soft, almost invisible in the misty morning chill, harsh and austere in the heat of the day and warmly seductive in the last evening light.

Ngorongoro is the dazzling jewel in northern Tanzania's peerless game-viewing circuit. Some 25 000 plains grazers reside within the crater – roughly 100 per square kilometre. Wildebeest, zebra and buffalo are most numerous, but there are also Thomson's and Grant's gazelle, Defassa water-buck, eland and bushbuck. The crater provides sanctuary to northern Tanzania's last few black rhinos, while serving as something of a retirement home for elephant bulls weighed down by tusks of a size seldom seen elsewhere. It also supports Africa's densest lion concentrations, though the dominant carnivore is the spotted hyena, some 400 of which prey on the abundant grazers. Remarkably, ecologist Hans Kruuk estimates that the Ngorongoro lions scavenge up to 80 per cent of their food from hyena kills.

ABOVE: Impressive tuskers are a feature of well-wooded parts of the crater floor.
BELOW: A bat-eared fox nudges its cubs.
OPPOSITE ABOVE: The forested rim of Lake Magadi.
OPPOSITE BELOW: Large flocks of flamingos often gather at Lake Magadi.

The endless plain

THE SERENGETI-MARA ECOSYSTEM

The elevated plains that sprawl northwest from the base of the Ngorongoro Highlands towards the Lake Victoria basin host what is surely Africa's most famous conservation area. This, of course, is the legendary Serengeti National Park, the 14 763-square-kilometre centrepiece of a virtually intact cross-border ecosystem. The ecosystem incorporates several other reserves, including parts of the Ngorongoro Conservation Area and Kenya's legendary Maasai Mara.

Neither bounded in by fences, nor pocketed off by encroaching cultivation, the Serengeti ecosystem is extraordinary in modern Africa in that it is defined by an ancient migration route, one followed annually by at least two million head of game – predominantly wildebeest, but also zebra, Thomson's gazelle, Grant's gazelle, topi, Coke's hartebeest and eland. Whether or not this would have been the most substantial migration of its kind before gun-happy Europeans arrived in Africa is anybody's guess. What is certain is that nothing on a comparable scale occurs anywhere else on Earth today.

The name Serengeti derives from the Maasai Serengit, meaning 'Endless Plain', which originally referred to the vast tracts of open grassland that characterize the southeast of the national park. This grassland spills over into the neighbouring Ngorongoro Conservation Area – part of the original national park as it was proclaimed in 1951, but de-gazetted eight years later in response to Maasai protests at being evicted from their traditional grazing grounds.

Serengeti National Park is more ecologically varied than many people realize. The Western Corridor, for instance, consists of broken savanna, interspersed with impenetrable stands of whistling thorns, and bisected by the perennial Grumeti River and a ribbon of riparian forest that harbours several species one wouldn't normally associate with the Serengeti. Among these species are the black-and-white colobus monkey, the eastern plantain-eater, Ross's Turaco, and the black-headed gonolek. Lobo, in the north, is probably the most conventionally scenic part of the Serengeti, all wooded hills and massive granite outcrops, while the open green grassland of Kenya's Maasai Mara Game Reserve – host to perhaps the densest predator concentrations anywhere in the ecosystem – is also unexpectedly hilly in parts.

OPPOSITE: The Serengeti-Mara ecosystem hosts one of the world's densest concentrations of large predators, such as the cheetah, as well as an abundance of wildebeest.
ABOVE: Among the scavenging beneficiaries of the numerous kills on the Serengeti-Mara plains are vultures, some six species of which are resident in the area.
OVERLEAF: The two-million-strong wildebeest migration through the Serengeti-Mara involves the crossing of the Mara River, where many weakened individuals fall prey to crocodile attacks.

183

RIGHT: As playful as
the domestic kitten it
so greatly resembles, a
young lion cub clings
affectionately to its
mother's tail.

RIGHT: As playful as the domestic kitten it so greatly resembles, a young lion cub clings affectionately to its mother's tail.

What all these different habitats have in common is that they are host to one of the world's great natural spectacles, the annual migration of millions of wildebeest in a column that can reach up to 40 kilometres in length. This migration follows a reasonably predictable annual cycle, depending on the exact timing and volume of the rains. The wildebeest typically spend about half of the year in the southeast plains of the national park, dispersing across the Seronera Plains at the start of the wet season, usually in late November, calving over January and February, and remaining until the end of the rains in late April or May.

The 800-kilometre northward migration, which usually commences in June, provides an annual bean feast to the Grumeti River's ravenous population of gargantuan crocodiles. The first animals to cross the river are most at risk, for which reason it can take up to two weeks from when the first herds arrive at the southern bank for the actual crossing to begin, by which time thousands upon thousands of wildebeest are congregated in the Western Corridor. From July to October, the ungulates disperse again, with about half of them tackling the equally risky crossing of the Mara River to enter Kenya's Maasai Mara Game Reserve, while the remainder disperse across the northern Serengeti. By late October, the animals have generally started to plod back southward to the Seronera Plains via Lobo, and the cycle starts all over again.

These immense ungulate herds provide rich pickings for the abundant and well-fed carnivores. Most numerous are spotted hyenas, which hunt their own prey with greater regularity than in many other parts of Africa. Lions also seem to be everywhere, idling away the daylight hours basking on rocks or in the short grass. More thinly distributed, leopards are often to be found lounging in the canopy of sausage trees and acacias along the Seronera River, while cheetahs favour the open grassland of the southeast. Among the more visible small predator species are bat-eared fox, serval and genet. This is also one of the few places where the ranges of all three African jackal species converge.

As the core of a migratory ecosystem that supports an estimated 2,5 million ungulates, the Serengeti is justifiably regarded as perhaps the finest of all African game reserves. But arguably the most memorable feature of the Serengeti are those wide oceans of grassland – cropped and yellow in the dry season, tall and green after the rains, punctuated by isolated archipelagos of granite koppies – and the soul-stirring sense of space alluded to in their Maasai name.

ABOVE: Burchell's zebra are the most populous grazers of the Serengeti-Mara after wildebeest and the two are often seen simultaneously.

LEFT: A pair of Red-billed Oxpeckers hitch a ride on the back of one of the very few black rhinos to survive in the Maasai Mara.

OVERLEAF: Lions pace across the plains of the Serengeti-Mara, watched nervously by a herd of grazing kongoni (Coke's hartebeest).

The Maasai

The archetypal East African pastoralists, the Maasai occupy one of the most extensive areas of any East African tribe, ranging across from central Tanzania through the Ngorongoro Highlands and Serengeti Plains to the Kenyan Rift Valley lakes of Naivasha and Nakuru. Yet they are relatively recent arrivals to the area. Oral traditions suggest that their forefathers migrated southward from the Sudanese Nile Valley in the fifteenth century and arrived in their present territory about 200 years later.

The Maasai are monotheists whose single deity has a dual nature – the benevolent Engai Narok (Black God) and vengeful Engai Nanyokie (Red God). They believe that Engai, who resides in the volcano Ol Doinyo L'Engai, made them the rightful owners of all the cattle in the world, a view that has occasionally made life difficult for neighbouring herders. Traditionally, this arrogance does not merely extend to cattle: agriculturist and fish-eating peoples are scorned, while Europeans' uptight clothing earned them the Maasai name *Iloredaa Enjekat* – 'Fart Smotherers!'

Like many East African pastoralists, the Maasai base their social structure on generational age-sets, the members of which are initiated at roughly the same time every 15 years or so, and consist of all the young men who have reached puberty and are not part of a previous age-set. In other words, initiates might be anything from 12 to 28 years old. When a new generation of warriors is initiated, the members of the previous generation graduate to junior elder status, and are responsible for all political and legislative decisions until they finally reach the rank of senior elders. Unlike Maasai girls, who are encouraged to marry as soon as they have been initiated, the members of any given warrior age-set must remain single until they are succeeded by a new generation.

The Maasai today remain immediately identifiable. The men drape themselves in toga-like red blankets, carry long wooden poles, and often dye their hair with red ochre and style it to look not unlike a Roman helmet. And while the women dress similarly to many other rural Tanzanians, their extensive use of beaded jewellery is highly distinctive. Today, the Maasai co-exist peacefully with their non-Maasai compatriots, but while their tolerance for their neighbours' idiosyncrasies has increased in recent decades, they show little interest in changing their own lifestyle.

ABOVE: Traditional Maasai knife and pouch.
BELOW: A Maasai moran (warrior) has his hair styled.
OPPOSITE: Maasai girls with their elaborate beadwork, facial dye and red blankets.
OVERLEAF: A Maasai woman tends her goats.

Where the monsoon winds blow

THE SWAHILI COAST

In 1331, the legendary Arab globetrotter Ibn Buttata, who travelled some 120 000 kilometres in his lifelong quest for fresh sights, alighted at an island-bound settlement he would later describe as 'one of the most beautiful and well-constructed towns in the world'. The name of that island, which supported a population of 10 000, was Kilwa – from AD 1150 to 1500 the most prosperous trade emporium on East Africa's luxuriant Swahili Coast.

The Swahili Coast – broadly speaking the Indian Ocean coastline from Mogadishu south to the Zambezi Delta – is endowed with an endless succession of picture-perfect beaches, the majority of which remain practically untouched by tourism. These idyllic expanses of soft white sand, hemmed in by swaying coconut palms and jungle-like coastal bush, are complemented by a series of offshore reefs whose kaleidoscopic swirls of fish have acquired legendary status with divers and snorkellers alike.

But the Swahili Coast also houses one of Africa's wealthiest architectural and cultural legacies: a series of sleepy ports and haunted ruins that document a maritime trade stretching back to Pharaonic times. This trade peaked following the seventh-century rise of Islam as, year after year, century after century, the monsoon winds blew dhows from Arabia and Asia into Kilwa, Mombasa, Malindi and dozens of lesser ports, to trade their exotic cargo for African wares such as ivory, ebony, tortoiseshell and, especially after 1000 AD, a bountiful supply of gold sourced from present-day Zimbabwe.

Kilwa presided over this so-called Golden Age of Swahili, which came to an abrupt end in 1505, when De Almeida's Portuguese war fleet arrived with all the self-righteous, murderous zeal of a religious crusade. Of the major Swahili city-states, only Malindi, whose rivalry with Mombasa pushed it into alliance with Portugal, was spared. Over subsequent centuries, trade ebbed and flowed, and individual ports flourished and declined, as first the Portuguese, then the Omani, and more recently the Germans and the British, held sway – but the Swahili Coast never quite recaptured its mediaeval pre-eminence.

Kilwa itself fell into virtual disuse after 1505. But its island-bound ruins, which stand off the southern mainland of present-day Tanzania, remain accessible by wind-borne dhows of a design practically unchanged in 1 000 years. The eleventh-century Great Mosque, notable for a finely executed and remarkably well-preserved ceiling of 16 cupolas, dominates the mediaeval town centre. Further east stand the flattened remains of a cliff-top palace that consisted of at least 100 rooms, a sunken audience court and a circular swimming pool. A large semi-collapsed fort on the island's landward shore is the sole relic of a brief eighteenth-century Omani reoccupation.

It would be easy to walk away from Kilwa, or any other contemporaneous coastal ruin, with the impression that it is an expression of a dead culture. But this is not so, for, while Swahili society, like any other, has evolved greatly since 1500, a strong sense of historical continuity binds the region to its illustrious past – as is evident in its picturesque timeworn backwaters. In Pangani, Bagamoyo, Saadani and Kilwa Kivinje, fishermen still lead a life ruled by the whimsical winds and tides of the ancient ocean.

If any part of the Swahili Coast presents a clear continuum between the mediaeval and the modern, it is Kenya's Lamu Archipelago, a constant, albeit peripheral, trade force throughout the last 1 000 years. The town of Lamu possesses an architectural

OPPOSITE: Practically unchanged in design for 1 000 years, the wooden dhows that ply East Africa's sleepy Indian Ocean coastline vary in size from the 20-metre-long *jahazi* to the 5-metre-long dugout *mtumbwi*, and are used both as public transport and as fishing vessels.
ABOVE: Traditional fishing methods, such as trawling with offshore nets, still predominate along the Swahili Coast.

195

OPPOSITE: Founded in the thirteenth century and designated a UNESCO World Heritage Site in 2001, the island-bound town of Lamu remains a compelling centre of Swahili traditionalism.

LEFT: A labyrinth of narrow, shadowy alleys runs between whitewashed houses, whose arched architecture reflects the strong Arabic influence on Swahili culture, as do the black *bui-bui* veils worn by the island's womenfolk (RIGHT).

BELOW: Traditional dhows still ply the modern waterfront.

OVERLEAF: Local fishermen examine the latest catch on an exquisite palm-lined beach outside Lindi in southern Tanzania.

197

integrity that borders on the spiritual: a compact labyrinth of shady, cobbled alleyways and tall whitewashed buildings where old Muslim men gossip on the pavements, young women draped in mysterious black veils glide in and out of ornate wooden doorways, and donkeys – still the main form of terrestrial transport – maintain their demented braying beneath the same pristine night sky that guided the mediaeval mariners.

A Swahili shipbuilding centre until it was captured by the Portuguese in 1510 to serve as their East African capital for almost 400 years, Mozambique Island protects the most important cluster of European architectural landmarks in sub-equatorial Africa. These landmarks include a church built in 1522, a formidable fortress constructed between 1556 and 1583, and a magnificent seventeenth-century Jesuit College. Yet the mood in its shadowy alleys, like those of Lamu, is overwhelmingly Islamic. In 1898, fol-

BELOW: The waterfront of Zanzibar's Stone Town, though more modern than Lamu, is lined with buildings dating to the Omani and British occupations of the late nineteeth century.

lowing the relocation of the national capital to Maputo, the descendants of Mozambique Island's original Swahili inhabitants, who had been sidelined to the adjacent mainland since 1510, drifted back across the water. Four long centuries of Portuguese occupation were reduced to little more than a passing architectural escapade – testament indeed to the resilience of Swahili culture.

In 1698, the Sultanate of Oman captured Mombasa, reducing the Portuguese sphere of influence to present-day Mozambique. With the gold trade by then a hazy memory, the Omani initiated a new and altogether more gruesome epoch of commercial prosperity based on the capture and sale of Africans into slavery. By 1840, when Sultan Said of Oman relocated his capital to Zanzibar, some 100 000 Africans were being captured annually in the hinterland of lakes Victoria, Tanganyika and Malawi,

BELOW: A Swahili girl framed by a wooden louvred window in Zanzibar's Stone Town.
BOTTOM: Zanzibar is a major centre for Tingatinga – a vibrant fusion of exotic and indigenous art developed by the Makua artist Edward Tingatinga in the psychedelic sixties.

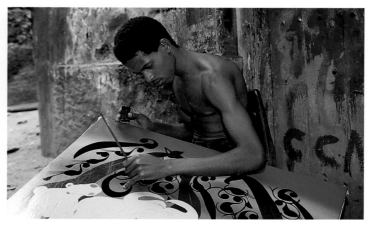

201

and shipped from mainland ports such as Bagamoyo, Pangani and Kilwa Kivinje for sale at Zanzibar's notorious slave market. Only in 1873 was Said's successor finally coerced into placing an absolute ban on the slave trade.

Who, exactly, are the Swahili? There's no simple answer. Their language is of the Bantu family, just like Zulu or Kikuyu but, as the long-serving *lingua franca* of coastal trade, its vocabulary borrows heavily from Arabic, Hindi and various European tongues. Ethnically, like modern Americans, the Swahili resist glib definition. They are the product of centuries of intermarriage between the original coastal inhabitants, Arabic and other settlers, and slaves imported or captured in the interior. Furthermore, historically the Swahili are urban traders, whose ports and cities were divided by large tracts of coast inhabited by other tribes. Who are the Swahili? As good an answer as any lies in the word's Arabic root 'Sahel', which translates, in this context, simply as 'coast'.

The strands that make up the Swahili Coast come together on Zanzibar, the magical 'spice island' that largely lives up to the exotic images its name evokes. Here, you'll find some of the most perfect beaches in creation, reefs teeming with colourful fish, the opportunity to swim with dolphins or to walk within metres of the endemic Kirk's red colobus monkey, and a clutch of overgrown ruins that collectively represent every phase of coastal history in the past 1 000 years. And then there is Zanzibar's legendary Stone Town – less isolated than its equivalent on Lamu – but nevertheless a fascinating time-worn enclave of traditional Swahili architecture and culture, set at the physical and spiritual heart of one of East Africa's most populous modern cities.

OPPOSITE: Kirk's red colobus, sporting a magnificent fringe, is one of Africa's most localized primates, restricted to a few relict forest patches on Zanzibar.
BELOW LEFT: Nutmeg is one of the many fragrant products grown on the 'Spice Island' of Zanzibar.
BELOW RIGHT: The biodiversity of shells of marine snails from around the African coast.
OVERLEAF: The endangered coconut or robber crab is the largest land crustacean in the world.

Great Zimbabwe and Kilwa

Of all the ruins that dot subequatorial Africa, none has the haunted resonance of Great Zimbabwe, the mediaeval stone city that rises from the rocky southern woodland of the country to which it has bequeathed its name. Like Kilwa, Great Zimbabwe supported some 10 000 inhabitants in its prime and, although many of the old stone houses have been reduced to rubble, its central features are extraordinarily well preserved. Among them is the Great Enclosure with its 5-metre-thick walls and 10-metre-high conical tower. This maze-like structure, built on a bare granite 'whaleback' was thought to have been a royal residence.

The first Europeans to visit Great Zimbabwe assumed it was the handiwork of Egyptians or Phoenicians or Arabs – anybody, that is, but indigenous 'black' Africans. And the popular notion that this magnificent stone edifice is the work of exotic settlers, though disproved conclusively in 1932, has never entirely died away, thanks to the former Rhodesian administration's stubborn insistence on peddling the ruined city's mysterious origins.

Many unanswered questions do hang over Great Zimbabwe – its contemporary name, for instance, and the symbolism that informed its more striking features. However, there is nothing controversial about its origin. Built around AD 1200, Great Zimbabwe succeeded Mapungubwe (a stone city founded on the southern bank of the Limpopo 200 years earlier) as the capital of the indigenous African kingdom that controlled the mines that supplied gold to the Swahili port of Kilwa. The gold was mined near Great Zimbabwe, transported overland to the now-submerged port of Sofala via the Zambezi Valley, then shipped northward to Kilwa by local mariners.

The rise and fall of Kilwa and Great Zimbabwe mirror each other closely, and their economic interdependence was underscored in 1971 with the discovery of Kilwa-minted coins at Great Zimbabwe. Yet, oddly, these two cities – the most impressive mediaeval constructions in subequatorial Africa – bear no architectural resemblance to each other whatsoever. The probable explanation for this is that the rulers of Great Zimbabwe controlled the gold trade as far as the coast. It is unlikely that an Arab or Swahili trader ever set foot in the great city from whence poured more than 10 per cent of the world's gold supply.

ABOVE AND BELOW: Towering above the surrounding aloes, the Great Enclosure is the most imposing indigenous structure in southern Africa. OPPOSITE: The mangrove-lined shore of the island (TOP) and the moody multi-domed Great Mosque at Kilwa (BELOW).

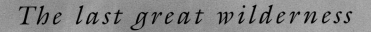

The last great wilderness

SOUTHERN TANZANIA

The Rufiji and its tributaries, the Great Ruaha and Kilombero, form the most extensive river system of the East African coastal belt. They provide a much-needed flow of perennial water through the hot, dry and tsetse-fly-ridden Brachystegia woodland of southern Tanzania. This water is vital to the wildlife protected within two of Africa's largest and most remote wilderness ecosystems, centred respectively on the Selous Game Reserve and the Ruaha National Park.

Named after a septuagenarian hunter-turned-soldier who was killed there by German fire towards the end of World War I, the 48 000-square-kilometre Selous is the largest game reserve in Africa, comparable in size to the combined area of the Kruger, Hwange and Serengeti national parks. A United Nations Educational, Scientific and Cultural Organization (UNESCO) World Heritage Site since 1982, it lies at the core of the 155 000-square-kilometre Greater Selous-Niassa Ecosystem, an incomparably vast chunk of African bush that also embraces Mikumi and Udzungwa national parks, the Kilombero Game Protected Area and Mozambique's Niassa Game Reserve.

Selous-Niassa supports an enormous mammal biomass. The elephant population, which declined from 110 000 to 25 000 during the 1980s because of intensive ivory poaching, now stands at 65 000, more than 5 per cent of the global total. Selous itself is home to at least 100 000 buffalo and 8 000 sable antelope, the greatest surviving concentrations of these animals in the world, as well as 40 000 hippo and 4 000 lion. An estimated 1 300 African wild dogs occur here, representing 25 per cent of the free-ranging population of this critically endangered canid, while the flood plain of the Kilombero River supports 70 per cent of the global population of the puku antelope.

Flanked by a labyrinth of hippo-infested channels, small lakes and swampy islets, the meandering Rufiji is the lifeblood of the Selous and an utterly compelling wildlife magnet: sandbanks are lined with outsized crocs; thirsty elephant, giraffe and buffalo herds mass on palm-fringed banks; and the muddy waters teem with grunting hippos. Lions are much in evidence, too, thanks to an unusual diurnal hunting strategy that involves resting near the riverbank to nab any thirsty ungulate unfortunate enough to stray within pouncing distance.

The Rufiji is a fine showcase for Africa's water birds, among them pairs of African Fish Eagles, Palm-nut Vultures standing sentinel on tall riverside borassus palms, flocks of Carmine Bee-eaters swirling decorously around the tall mud banks in which they nest, or shorebirds such as Yellow-billed Storks, Spur-winged Plovers and African Skimmers.

OPPOSITE: A lioness gorges herself on a fresh buffalo kill in the Selous Game Reserve.
ABOVE: Once common and widespread throughout the continent, the African wild dog (also known as the hunting or painted dog) is now regarded as endangered, thanks to persecution by farmers and to diseases spread by domestic dogs. Its most important stronghold today is the Selous Game Reserve, whose estimated 1 300 individuals represent roughly one-quarter of the global wild population.

ABOVE: Lush vegetation and sparkling waterfalls characterize the Udzungwa Mountains in southern Tanzania.

Bulbous, ancient baobab silhouettes haunt the semi-arid plains and rocky slopes of Ruaha National Park, which is bordered by the Ruaha River, a tributary of the Rufiji. This park also boasts an enviable mammal checklist. Cheetahs and leopards are conspicuous, as are prides of 20-odd lions – capable of reducing a large male buffalo to a skeleton in a couple of hours – and at least two resident packs of African wild dogs.

Ruaha is transitional to the southern miombo and northern savanna biomes, and its impressive number of antelope species includes Grant's gazelle and lesser kudu (at the very south of their range), as well as more significant numbers of sable, roan and greater kudu than occur anywhere further north. Impala, waterbuck, bushbuck, buffalo, zebra and giraffe are all common, while some 12 000 elephant are resident within the greater Ruaha ecosystem, which includes several neighbouring game reserves.

The most remote and least heralded of southern Tanzania's savanna reserves, Katavi National Park is set in the shallow and thinly populated sub-branch of the Rift Valley that terminates in the swampy expanse of Lake Rukwa. A classic dry-season reserve, Katavi is practically impenetrable during the rains, which transform its black-cotton soil into a mosquito- and tsetse-infested quagmire. By contrast, when the swamps subside, the only reliable water sources for miles around are a couple of improbably feeble streams that run through a wide grassy flood plain and attract incredible concentrations of game. Lion and elephant are numerous, and thousand-strong buffalo herds regularly amass on the plains alongside Defassa waterbuck, topi, impala and zebra. Most remarkable of all, however, are the pods of up to 200 hippos that jostle for wallowing space in practically any stretch of water more than a few inches deep.

ABOVE: During the dry season, aggregations of up to 200 hippopotamuses wallow in the riverine pools that run through the flood plains of Katavi National Park.

Big cats

Perhaps it has something to do with their resemblance to overgrown domestic cats, possibly it's simply because our ancestors expended so much time and effort keeping out of their way, who knows? But whatever the reason, there's no doubting the fact that Africa's big cats exude a singular – some might say primal – fascination over all who are fortunate enough to encounter them in the wild.

The guaranteed showstopper on any first safari is the lion, Africa's largest predator, a powerful tawny feline that typically lives in family units of 5 to 10 animals – though prides of 20-plus are a feature of Ruaha and the Maasai Mara. Lions spend up to 23 hours of any given day lounging around in regal indolence. Hunting is generally a collaborative nocturnal effort between females, who favour medium-sized antelope such as impala, though in some areas buffaloes and even giraffe are regularly taken. Rivalry between males is intense: battles to take over a pride are frequently fought to the death, and male cubs are usually killed after a successful takeover bid.

A solitary and secretive nocturnal hunter, the leopard tends to stick to dense vegetation and rocky slopes, where it still often persists in close proximity to humans without ever being seen. Distinguished by a stocky build and beautiful golden coat broken up by distinctive black rosettes, the leopard is Africa's most widespread and numerous big cat, but is seldom seen more than fleetingly, except where individuals have become habituated to vehicles. For this reason it is the feline most eagerly sought by those in the know.

The only feline to lack retractable claws, the cheetah is an aberrant spotted cat whose greyhound-like build is ideally suited to chasing down small to medium-sized antelope in open savanna habitats. Indeed, it is the world's fastest land animal, capable of exceeding 70 kilometres per hour in short bursts. Despite superficial similarities, the cheetah can easily be distinguished from the leopard by its simple (as opposed to rosette) spots, disproportionately small head, streamlined build, diagnostic black tear marks, and preference for relatively open habitats.

ABOVE: The lion is the largest of Africa's cats, but it lacks the agility of the more arboreal leopard (BELOW). Both are considerably more bulky than the cheetah (OPPOSITE), which can be distinguished from other spotted cats by the black 'tear marks' that run between its eyes and mouth.

SOUTHERN
AFRICA

In the popular imagination, North Africa is inexorably linked with the sandy Sahara, West Africa with the rainforests of the Congo Basin, and East Africa with the game-rich savanna that flanks the Great Rift Valley – simplistic images, for sure, but ones that do nevertheless define the geographical essence of each region.

Southern Africa is different. Certainly, the region has its geographic icons, whether it is the mighty white-water rush of Victoria Falls, the curvaceous red dune fields of Sossusvlei, or the imposing sandstone bulk of Table Mountain overshadowing Cape Town. But pin a map on a wall, toss a dart, and you'll find that the essence of southern Africa falls somewhere between the barren thirstland of the Kalahari, the Mediterranean-style vineyards that flourish beneath the Cape Fold Mountains, the palm-lined beaches of KwaZulu-Natal, and the hippo-infested channels of the Zambezi.

Despite its immense ecological variety, southern Africa displays strong general climatic patterns, which are influenced by the combination of altitude, ocean currents and distance from the equator. The west is generally far drier and more lightly vegetated than the east – indeed much of Namibia, Botswana and the northwest of South Africa consists of desert or semi-desert – while temperatures tend to rise as one heads further north into the Brachystegia woodland that characterizes Zimbabwe, Zambia and Malawi.

Several of the continent's finest game reserves can be found within southern Africa – Kruger, Hwange, Etosha, Chobe and South Luangwa to name but a few – and are at the centre of its booming tourist industry. Ironically, however, it is the drier and somewhat more game-depleted west that attracts the attention of ecologists. At least 5 000 plant species are confined to the Western Cape,

OPPOSITE: Situated on the border of Zambia and Zimbabwe, the mile-wide Victoria Falls is widely regarded to be the most impressive phenomenon of its type in the world.

Karoo and Kalahari, and this region is also the main stronghold for the majority of the 280 reptile and 62 bird species that are endemic or near-endemic to South Africa – a country that the World Conservation Monitoring Service has ranked third in the world in terms of overall biodiversity.

In cultural terms, southern Africa is the least overtly traditional part of the continent, and probably the most outward looking. South Africa in particular boasts unusually high education standards and employment prospects – the national GDP is said to be roughly equivalent to that of the rest of sub-Saharan Africa combined – and over recent years it has transformed quite remarkably into a fully fledged democracy whose constitution can be regarded as enlightened by any standards.

BELOW: A Zulu mother and her two children wearing traditional garb watch the world go by outside their beehive hut.

Ironically, one factor in creating the relative prosperity and the cosmopolitan atmosphere which prevails in modern-day southern Africa has been the same high level of alien settlement that led to the creation of the policy of separate development of the races known as apartheid. The other is the fantastic mineral wealth that attracted a great many of those settlers to the country. Indeed, it is difficult to imagine how southern Africa might look today had it not been for the discovery of gold below present-day Johannesburg in 1886. Almost certainly, there would have been no Anglo-Boer War, no unionization of the former British colonies and Boer Republics that constitute the country we know as South Africa, and the regional economic powerhouse of Gauteng – with its nine million residents – might still be an undistinguished patch of highveld farmland.

BELOW: A male ostrich feeds on the rocky ground in the semi-arid Karoo. CENTRE: An isolated stand of baobab trees on Kubu Island in Botswana's Makgadikgadi Pans region. BOTTOM: Skittish Burchell's zebra flee across a waterhole in Namibia's Etosha Pan.

217

River of thunder
THE ZAMBEZI

The local Makalolo people know it as Mosi-oa-Tunya: The Smoke that Thunders. David Livingstone, the first European to see it, renamed it – somewhat more prosaically – in honour of his queen. But whatever you might choose to call it, few would deny that Victoria Falls is one of the world's most awesome natural phenomena. This 2-kilometre-wide sheet of water is formed by the Zambezi as it crashes over a 100-metre-high precipice on the Zambia-Zimbabwe border.

In the peak months of February and March the Falls carry up to 500 000 cubic metres of water per minute and kick up a rainbow-tinted, 500-metre-high plume of spray that is visible 80 kilometres away. Victoria Falls is roughly double the height and width of Niagara Falls, and considerably less tainted by human ornament and artifice. Indeed, as seen today from any of several lushly forested and spray-doused viewpoints, Victoria Falls looks practically as unspoilt as it would have on 16 November 1855, when an overawed Livingstone suggested that 'scenes so lovely must have been gazed upon by angels in their flight'.

Africa's fourth-longest river, the Zambezi flows for almost 3 000 kilometres from its source in northwestern Zambia into a wide delta some 200 kilometres north of Beira. Its drainage basin, which includes tributaries such as the Chobe, Shire, Kafue, Luangwa and Gwayi, covers more than 1.3 million square kilometres, centred on Zambia and Zimbabwe, but also extends into parts of Angola, Mozambique, Malawi, Botswana, Namibia and Tanzania.

The Zambezi feeds two vast artificial lakes formed by hydroelectric dams: Kariba on the Zimbabwe-Zambia border and Cahora Bassa in Mozambique. Downstream of these dams, the Zambezi is in turn fed – via the Shire River – by the continent's third-largest and arguably most beautiful freshwater body. This is the 585-kilometre-long Lake Nyasa (Lake Malawi), where deep aquamarine water – hemmed in by the towering escarpment of the southern Rift Valley – laps white sandy beaches lined with baobabs from where African Fish Eagles utter eerie, evocative calls.

The Zambezi Basin lies at the core of the Miombo Belt, which is sometimes also referred to as the Zambezian Biome, and consists of a wide ribbon of tall deciduous broad-leaved woodland that divides the acacia savanna of East Africa from similar thornbush habitats further south. Dominated by the leguminous tree genera *Brachystegia*, *Julbernardia* and *Isoberlinia*, this belt forms an important stronghold for several large mammal species, such as sable and roan antelope and side-striped jackal, while a full 67 bird species are regarded as endemic to miombo woodland.

OPPOSITE: A herd of buffalo on the shores of the Zambezi River.
BELOW: Canoes ply the stretch of the Zambezi between the Kariba and Cahora Bassa dams.

The Zambezi Basin hosts some of Africa's most compelling game-viewing territory, including a trio of superb national parks. There is Zambia's little visited Kafue National Park, which extends over 22 500 square kilometres, making it the largest national park on the continent. Also in Zambia, South Luangwa National Park is known for dense concentrations of grazers on the Luangwa River in the dry season, as well as superb nocturnal viewing of leopard, genet and porcupine, among others. Finally, there is Botswana's Chobe National Park. The rainy season in Chobe is the focal point of one of southern Africa's most important remaining migratory ecosystems: some 35 000 elephants cross annually into Hwange National Park in western Zimbabwe.

Down-river of Kariba, Zambia's Lower Zambezi National Park and Zimbabwe's Mana Pools flank a maze of forest-fringed channels set below a craggy southern arm of the Rift Valley known as the Zambezi Escarpment. Dotted with sand bars and islands, this lush riverine wilderness has a magical, untouched atmosphere: hippos splutter and yawn around every bed, gigantic crocodiles slither menacingly through the clear water, lions and leopards prowl the thickets in search of prey, and venerable elephant bulls forage methodically in shady riverbank groves. Explored by canoe, it is the ultimate Zambezian wildlife experience – and arguably the most thrilling riverine game viewing to be had anywhere in Africa.

BELOW: In the ultimate clash of the African titans, an agitated elephant decides somewhat emphatically that it doesn't feel like sharing its water-hole – set in Botswana's Chobe National Park – with a pesky pride of lions.

LEFT: A flock of Red-billed Queleas.
TOP: The gem-like Malachite Kingfisher.
CENTRE: The gaudy Livingstone's Turaco.
ABOVE: The African Darter.
OVERLEAF: Zebra and wildebeest graze in a seasonal flood plain in Hwange National Park.

223

Okavango

Southern Africa's third-longest river, the Kavango, rises in central Angola, flows south through Namibia's Caprivi Strip, then fans out into the northern Kalahari to form a vast inland delta called the Okavango, before it literally vanishes into thin air. Some 95 per cent of the water that flows into the delta is lost to evaporation, with the remainder either being swallowed by the thirsty desert sands or exiting the delta via its sole outlet, the Thamalakane River.

Extending over 16 000 square kilometres, the delta's mesmerizing maze of ever-shifting channels and islets – best explored in a type of dugout known locally as a *makoro* – hosts a prolific cast of aquatic and non-aquatic creatures. Hippos and crocodiles are abundant in the lily-covered channels, while fringing papyrus beds provide an important refuge to the splay-hoofed sitatunga antelope. The islands support elephant, buffalo, zebra, and a wide variety of carnivores and antelope including the localized red lechwe and puku.

The delta is something of a showcase for Africa's aquatic bird life. It is an important breeding site for the endangered Wattled Crane, and provides sanctuary to a variety of storks as well as 18 heron species, including the largest breeding population of the range-restricted Slaty Egret. Other key water-associated birds include the Pygmy Goose, Long-toed Plover, Pel's Fishing-Owl, Coppery-tailed Coucal, Swamp Boubou and Rosy-throated Longclaw.

The Kavango originally terminated in a large shallow lake that extended between present-day Lake Ngami and the Makgadikgadi Pans. This basin dried up some 10 000 years ago, as a result of a slight shift in local tectonic gradients, exacerbated by an accumulation of silt washed down from what is today Angola. The delta remains a highly dynamic ecosystem. It is subject to regular changes in course, which are linked to rainfall levels in Angola, silting up and vegetation blockage, as well as low-scale tectonic activity.

ABOVE: A subsistence Beyei fisherman of the Okavango Delta.
BELOW: Roosting bee-eaters.
OPPOSITE ABOVE: The islands and waterways of the central Okavango wilderness area.
OPPOSITE BELOW: The semi-aquatic red lechwe.

The great thirstland
THE KALAHARI

It's no place for agoraphobics, the Northern Cape. Accounting for some 30 per cent of South Africa's surface area, making it significantly larger than Great Britain, the Northern Cape's population of fewer than one million people is just 1,8 per cent of the national tally. And this population figure is actually distorted *upward* by the inclusion in the provincial border of Kimberley, the city whose famous 'Big Hole' was the focal point of the Victorian diamond rush that kickstarted the career of Cecil John Rhodes, among others.

The borders of the Northern Cape coincide loosely with those of the Karoo and Kalahari biomes, whose sandy, thinly vegetated soils extend northward from the Cape winelands all the way through to southern Angola. For many people, this arid part of South Africa feels like hell on Earth, and certainly it's not a place where you'd want to find yourself stranded without transport or drinking water. But for aficionados of the southern savanna, there's nowhere quite like the Kalahari – with the magnitude of its horizons, the implacable sense of emptiness that broods over its red dunes and haggard rockscapes, and a night sky so vast and bright it might be alive.

The Northern Cape would be an emptier place still were it not for the fact that, ironically, South Africa's largest river, the Orange, runs right through its parched heart. It provides a vital source of water to towns such as Upington, whose defiantly well-groomed lawns come as a shock after driving through the surrounding thirstland. Founded in the nineteenth century as an isolated mission station, Upington owes its recent growth to the ambitious irrigation scheme that follows the course of the Orange. The fruits of this scheme can be tasted at the world's second-largest wine co-op, producer of more than 100 000 tons annually.

The most memorable feature of the Orange lies down-river of Upington: Augrabies Falls, whose name derives from a Bushman phrase that translates as 'Place of Great Noise'. It's not the height of Augrabies that is so impressive, nor is it the racket made by South Africa's largest river as it tumbles over a 56-metre cliff into the base of an 18-kilometre-long canyon, rather it is the thrilling perversity of a waterfall of this magnitude being set in an otherwise bleak moonscape of flat sandy soil broken by bulbous black granite outcrops. A remarkable plant associated with this area is the kokerboom (quiver tree), a tall, spindly aloe, the name of which derives from the old Bushman custom of using the hollowed-out stem as a quiver to hold a bow and arrows.

OPPOSITE: A dirt track runs through the vast emptiness of Botswana's Makgadikgadi Pans.
BELOW: Donkey carts are a common mode of transport in South Africa's Northern Cape province.

ABOVE: At Augrabies, known to the Bushmen as 'Place of Great Noise', the Orange River, South Africa's largest waterway, plunges violently into a 56-metre-deep gorge.

OPPOSITE: The kokerboom, or quiver tree, is a large, distinctive aloe whose range is virtually confined to the Kalahari of the South Africa-Namibia border area.

Rather more typical of the watercourses of the Kalahari are the Auob and Nossob, which run – but very seldom flow – through the 350 000-square-kilometre Kgalagadi Transfrontier Park, an amalgamation of South Africa's Kalahari Gemsbok National Park and its near namesake, the Gemsbok National Park in Botswana. Kgalagadi protects a fragile dune ecosystem bounded by the dry, camelthorn-lined beds of the Auob and Nossob, a harsh and uncompromising environment where human intruders become keenly aware of the precarious balance between life and death. Yet, paradoxically, Kgalagadi is also a reserve of singular beauty, with its trademark red dunes set against a constant cloudless blue sky.

This seemingly inhospitable tract of parched sand is inhabited by several species adapted to arid environments. The handsome gemsbok, for instance, is unique among mammals in being able to tolerate a body temperature of 45 degrees Celsius, which means that it doesn't need to lose water in the form of sweat. In common with the springbok, the gemsbok feeds mainly in the cool early morning, when the moisture

The Kalahari supports a range of species adapted to its arid climate: the suricate, or meerkat (OPPOSITE), which often stands upright to gain a wider view of the area; the bat-eared fox (LEFT) which has adapted to the local climate by hunting nocturnally in summer and diurnally in winter, and the springbok (BELOW), seen here suckling a two-week-old lamb.

content of plants is highest, and it can supplement its everyday diet by eating the juicy tsamma melons that grow in the dunes. The carnivores of Kgalagadi also display some unusual adaptations. The brown hyena, for instance, frequently hoards ostrich eggs as a source of both nutrition and liquid, while the park's bat-eared foxes alternate their hunting habits seasonally, being almost exclusively diurnal in winter, when night-time temperatures frequently drop below freezing, but reverting to nocturnal foraging during the searing summer months.

It seems scarcely credible that humans could survive without artificial assistance in this harsh environment. But they can – indeed, until very recently, significant numbers actually did. As testified to by such names as Kgalagadi, Augrabies and tsamma, the Kalahari provided a last refuge to the Khoisan-speaking hunter-gatherers – widely referred to as Bushmen or San, though both terms originated as derogatory appellations – who inhabited most of southern Africa until about 2 000 years ago. Gradually, these

BELOW: A sheep farm in the Northern Cape. The Kalahari, as well as the more southerly Karoo, are well known for the fine lamb and mutton produced on their ranches.

slightly built hunter-gatherers were displaced by Bantu-speaking pastoralist and agriculturalist migrants from the north, but they were able to hold their own in arid or montane areas unsuited to cattle-rearing or growing crops, because of their traditional knowledge of wildlife and skill at locating subterranean or vegetable sources of water.

Recent centuries have been cruel to the so-called Bushmen – persecuted as vermin by black pastoralists and white settlers, then evicted from their home territories by conservationists, coerced into abandoning their traditional ways, or seduced by introduced vices such as alcohol and marijuana. A few thousand individuals still inhabit basic settlements verging on the Kgalagadi (mainly in Namibia, but also in South Africa and Botswana), but levels of substance abuse are high, poverty is rife, few individuals still know how to hunt or to gather for a living, and the click-based Khoisan language is dying a gradual death – shockingly, not one living South African is fluent in this most ancient of the country's documented tongues.

OVERLEAF: Kalahari Bushmen congregate below a spreading acacia tree – complete with sociable weaver nest – before setting off to hunt.

Madagascar

Madagascar, situated some 400 kilometres offshore of Mozambique, supports the world's most radical island ecology. Roughly 90 per cent of the plants that occur there naturally are unique, as are 225 reptile species, 105 bird species, and countless invertebrate species. In addition, its mammalian fauna represents something akin to a living ecological fossil – bats aside, every last mammal genus is endemic. Collectively, this fauna is far closer to the African fauna of 50 million years ago than to its modern counterpart.

The most celebrated Malagasy endemics are the lemurs, which are long-tailed, mostly arboreal primates of which more than 50 species have been identified. Lemurs are classified as prosimians, a suborder of primates that thrived globally between 60 and 35 million years ago, since when – exceptions such as the bushbabies notwithstanding – it has been superseded by the more recently evolved monkey and ape orders. Other unusual Malagasy mammals include the fossa, a dog-sized carnivore related to mongooses and civets, and more than 20 species of insectivorous tenrecs, regarded to be the most primitive living mammals by some biologists.

Madagascar's unique biology is a product of the same tectonic plate activity responsible for the Rift Valley. The island split from the African mainland about 140 million years ago, at which time mammals were poorly evolved. Lemurs and the like probably crossed at a later date on rafts of floating vegetation. Eventually – at least 30 million years ago – the island drifted too far for any terrestrial mammals to reach it from the mainland, and the channel would have become an increasingly substantial obstacle to the more mobile bats and birds.

The latest mammalian arrivals to Madagascar probably washed up about 2 000 years ago, after having sailed across from southeast Asia. Since then, human activity has caused the extinction of several endemics, including a type of lemur as large as a gorilla, and a flightless bird that stood a metre taller than an ostrich. Sadly, with more than half the forest that existed in 1950 now gone, further extinctions seem certain to follow.

ABOVE: Parson's chameleon is one of more than 200 reptile species which are unique to Madagascar.
BELOW: The rainforests of Madagascar are constantly being reduced as a result of clearance by subsistence farmers seeking fresh land to plant their crops.
OPPOSITE: Verreaux's sifaka is capable of short bursts of bipedal locomotion.

The living desert
NAMIBIA

More thinly populated than even the Northern Cape, with just 1.6 million people scattered across an area larger than the United Kingdom and Germany combined, Namibia must rank close to being the emptiest non-polar nation on the planet. Spectacularly so, for while much of the countryside is too desiccated and desolated to sit comfortably with adjectives such as pretty or beautiful, there is a sheer vastness to the Namibian landscape that is at once humbling, breathtaking – and profoundly liberating.

The northeastern savanna is the most stereotypically African of the country's four main geographic zones. Snuggled up against the Angolan border, it receives an average annual rainfall in excess of 500 millimetres – generous by Namibian standards – and supports by far its densest human concentrations. The remainder of the country is arid or semi-arid, breaking up into three zones: the Kalahari along the eastern border with Botswana, the Namib Desert along the western coastal belt, and the narrow and relatively fertile elevated escarpment that divides them.

Namib-Naukluft National Park is the more southerly of two vast reserves that protect the desert of the coastal belt. The desert's arid climate is determined by the combination of warm, dry winds from the interior blowing across the Atlantic's cold Benguela Current, conditions that discourage evaporation and the formation of rain-bearing clouds. As a result, the Namib receives a paltry annual average rainfall of 15 millimetres, and some areas might go years without receiving a single drop of rain.

The same hot, dry winds have moulded the characteristic 'scorpion-tails' of the red dunes around Sossusvlei on the western border of Namib-Naukluft. Here, the world's tallest dunes – rippled apricot mountains formed not from local soil, but, bizarrely, from red sand blown across from the Kalahari – tower above a series of parched seasonal pans. These pans might fill up with water for a month only once or twice per decade. The most famous – and most photographed – of these is Dead Pan. Its cracked floor of dried mud supports a spectral forest of camelthorn trunks that died some 500 years ago, when this weird Hadean lake last received water on a regular basis.

OPPOSITE: A Himba woman leans against the elementary hut that provides her only shelter from the harsh climatic conditions of the northern Namibian desert.
BELOW: The cracked bed of one of the parched pans that lie below the dunes of Sossusvlei.
OVERLEAF: Some of the world's largest dunes are to be found in the Sossusvlei sector of the Namib-Naukluft National Park in Namibia.

241

Reptiles

Ever since that legendary serpentine encounter in the Garden of Eden, reptiles have tended to receive bad press, much of it rather unfair. The most visible African reptiles are lizards such as the common house gecko: endearing bug-eyed, translucent white midgets that scamper up walls and ceilings to satisfy their voracious appetite for insects. Snakes also play an important natural role in vermin control, while their retiring nature means that they account for far fewer human deaths than is often supposed. In South Africa, for instance, lightning is probably a bigger killer!

The majority of African snakes are non-venomous and harmless to any creature much larger than a rat – one exception being the 5-metre-long rock python, whose muscular body can asphyxiate a small antelope. Of the venomous snakes, the most deadly is the puff adder, not because it is especially venomous, but because of a sluggish disposition that makes it more likely to be disturbed than other species. By contrast, the non-aggressive and back-fanged boomslang, despite being exceptionally toxic, is not on record as ever having killed a person in the wild.

The most intriguing of African reptiles are the true chameleons, whose legendary ability to change colour is influenced by mood more than by physical background. Two remarkable physiological features common to all true chameleons are protuberant eyes that offer 180-degree vision on both sides and swivel independently, and a body-length tongue that can be unleashed in a blink-and-you'll-miss-it lunge at a selected item of prey. Many chameleons are adorned with facial casques, horns and crests that enhance their already prehistoric appearance.

Truly prehistoric, the Nile crocodile is the largest representative of the 150-million-year-old order Crocodilia, regularly attaining a length of 6 metres, and remarkably similar to ancestral species that lived contemporaneously with dinosaurs. An opportunistic feeder, it feeds mostly on fish, but will also take drinking or swimming mammals – humans included. The Nile crocodile is still common in most conservation areas; some truly gargantuan specimens haunt the sandbanks of the Victoria Nile, Lower Zambezi and Rufiji.

ABOVE: The horned Johnstone's chameleon is endemic to the highland forests of central East Africa.
BELOW: Measuring up to 1,35 metres, the dragon-like rock monitor is Africa's second-largest lizard after the closely related Nile monitor.
OPPOSITE: The mildly venomous horned adder is distinguished by the presence of its single horn above each eye.

A black-backed jackal (OPPOSITE ABOVE) is too small to concern a giraffe drinking at a waterhole in Namibia's legendary Etosha Pan National Park. But this small canid is certainly swift and stealthy enough to surprise a flock of doves (OPPOSITE BELOW), and successfully capture one of its number (ABOVE AND BELOW), an important source of protein during the dry season.

The combination of the crisp, clear desert air and absence of competing light sources makes the Namib night sky a thing of shimmering, awe-inspiring beauty. No less memorable is the silence of the Namib on a windless night – so close to absolute that it becomes almost tangible, barely intruded upon by birdcalls or the white noise of insects, but sporadically broken by the gentle chatter of the barking gecko and occasional distant whooping of a jackal or a hyena.

The Namib supports a low volume of wildlife, with gemsbok perhaps the most common large mammal, often to be seen filing nobly across the crest of a dune. The scanty vegetable cover does, however, include the truly national plant *Welwitschia mirabilis*. This ground-hugging form of conifer consists of just one stumpy, spongy stem and two long serrated leaves that grow – over thousands of years – into windblown tangles, reminiscent of a stranded heap of seaweed.

In the far northwest of Namibia, the rocky 95 000 square kilometre wilderness known as Damaraland or the Kaokoveld is home to a distinct desert race of black rhinos. They routinely cover more than 50 kilometres in one day in search of water. This remote corner of Namibia is also home to the world's only population of desert-adapted elephants – animals that obtain water by digging into subterranean streams. The streams shadow watercourses that might flow above ground for only a few hours annually after a flash flood.

BELOW: A lioness trips a young kudu in Etosha. OPPOSITE: The supreme desert antelope is the gemsbok (or southern oryx), seen here strolling through the inhospitable plains of the Namib-Naukluft National Park. OVERLEAF: A mixed herd of giraffe, greater kudu, Burchell's zebra and springbok congregate at a waterhole in Etosha.

BELOW: A family group of
ostriches – which are the
world's largest birds, but
are too heavy to fly – jog
across the arid plains below
the dunes of Sossusvlei.

Namibia's small population includes several minorities who still adhere to a greater
or lesser degree to their traditional lifestyles, for example, the Bushmen in and around
the Kalahari. The most charismatic of the country's Bantu-speakers are the Himba of
the Kaokoveld, a staunchly pastoral people whose ochre-red, braided hairstyles, costumes of hides and beads, and love of cattle recall the desert-dwelling pastoralists of the
Ethiopia-Kenya border area.

The relatively moist area north of Namibia is home to one of southern Africa's most
lauded game reserves, the immense Etosha Pan National Park, named after a seasonal

pan of 6 000 square kilometres, which held permanent water until about two million years ago, but now stands empty for most of the year, like a shimmering white and relentlessly flat mirage. Etosha is most popular in the dry season, when a string of natural and artificial waterholes along the southern rim of the pan attract prodigious mixed grazing herds, as well as the predators that feed on them. Coming from elsewhere in this parched land, however, the incongruity of Etosha in the rainy season, with its waterlogged green fields littered with yellow wild flowers and alive with fawning antelope, is in itself rather miraculous.

BELOW: Cormorants nest on a shipwreck along Namibia's treacherous Skeleton Coast.
BOTTOM: Cape fur seals are prolific at Cape Cross.

Elephants

The world's largest terrestrial mammal, the African elephant can grow to be 4 metres high and a large bull might weigh in at 6 000 kilograms. This iconic giant is the sole remaining African representative of a lineage that first appears in the fossil record some 35 million years ago. Then it was an antelope-sized aquatic creature, whose small trunk and tusks were prototypes of the two features that most distinguish its modern descendants. Interestingly, fossil evidence suggests that the familiar savanna race of elephant *Loxodonta africana africana* is a relatively recent variation on the smaller and slightly hairier *Loxodonta africana cyclotis* of the West African rainforest. Until about 20 000 years ago, the dominant elephant of the savanna belonged to the extinct genus *Elephas*.

Highly intelligent and reliably entertaining, the African elephant lives in close-knit female-dominated clans consisting of the eldest (matriarch) cow and her sisters, daughters and grand-daughters. Mother-daughter bonds are strong and may exist for up to 50 years. Males generally leave the family group at around 12 years, after which they either roam around alone or form bachelor herds. Under normal circumstances, elephants range widely in search of food and water, but concentrated populations confined within conservation areas can wreak havoc on the environment.

Ivory hunting caused elephants to become extinct in North Africa during Roman times. It is also responsible for a severe depletion in their numbers elsewhere on the continent, often exacerbated by the arrival of European traders or settlers. Nevertheless, the continental population probably stood at around five million prior to the wholesale slaughter perpetrated by commercial ivory poachers over the 1980s. A 1989 Convention for the International Trade in Endangered Species (CITES) moratorium on ivory sales has been instrumental in halting – and in many cases reversing – the trend, as perhaps have the improved economic and political circumstances in key countries such as Tanzania and Uganda. All the same, the most optimistic current continent-wide estimate is perhaps one million, and numbers are probably still in decline outside of those select conservation areas that afford elephants genuine protection.

Elephants frequently give themselves dust baths, both to cool down and to protect their wrinkled skins from parasites. They also consume vast amounts of water and a herd will typically spend an hour or two daily at a waterhole.

Named after the river that forms the border with Angola and provides the only source of drinking water for miles around, the Kunene region of the Namibian Kaokoveld is among the most remote and harsh of African landscapes. The Himba (OPPOSITE AND LEFT), who inhabit the area, are hardy pastoralists, whose staunch adherence to a traditional lifestyle echoes that of the Maasai or Afar of the East African Rift. The only wildlife capable of surviving this harsh climate consists of desert-adapted species, such as the gemsbok (BELOW).

257

Swaziland

The Kingdom of Swaziland, bounded on three sides by South Africa, is one of the very few modern African states where tribal and national identities amount to pretty much the same thing. This is because its borders approximate those of a valid pre-colonial polity. The centralized Swazi Kingdom was forged during the nineteenth-century regional shake-up initiated by the rise of Shaka Zulu further south.

Placed under British rule in the aftermath of the Anglo-Boer War, Swaziland only regained its independence in 1968 under King Sobhuza II. Yet, throughout this era, the Swazi retained an autonomous identity that would have been more easily undermined in a multi-tribal society. For instance, because the British recognized only one monarch – their own – they downgraded the Swazi king's title to paramount chief, but this didn't much impress his subjects, who returned the snub by failing to accord King George VI the Swazi royal salute when he visited in 1947.

The first Europeans to visit Swaziland encountered grazing herds that 'covered the land as far as the eye could see'. Then they opened fire, precipitating a gradual decline in the kingdom's once prolific wildlife. By 1960, you could drive the length of the Swaziland Lowveld, recalls conservationist Ted Reilly, and 'not see a single wild animal'. That Swaziland retains any wildlife today is largely due to the efforts of Reilly, who set aside his family farm to become the kingdom's first protected area in 1960, and who persuaded Sobhuza II to gazette his royal hunting ground at Hlane as a national park.

Today, a dozen private and state reserves are dotted around the kingdom. In the Lowveld, Hlane and Mkhaya – the latter also founded by Reilly – protect some of Africa's densest rhino populations. Further west, Malolotja Nature Reserve is Swaziland's last true wilderness area, with a mere 20 kilometres of roads traversing some 18 000 hectares of layered mountains and breezy grassland plateaux studded with blossoming proteas, the rare Barberton and Kaapsehoop cycads, and regional endemics such as black wildebeest, bontebok and bald ibis.

ABOVE: Waterfalls, such as this one at Phophonyane, characterize the escarpment of Swaziland.
BELOW: A Mantenga village with typical beehive huts.
OPPOSITE: A Swazi woman plays the makhoyane, or Swazi guitar.

Land of the rising sun

MPUMALANGA AND THE KRUGER NATIONAL PARK

In 1886, on the highveld farm of Langlaagte, an Australian prospector stumbled across an outcrop of what would turn out to be the richest gold reef ever discovered. Barely two years later, the surrounding farmland had mushroomed into a sprawling, crime-ridden shantytown of bars and brothels that ranked as the most populous – and rowdiest – settlement anywhere in southern Africa. And that much Johannesburg still is today – the high-rise, high-octane heart of a tiny urbanized province whose mineral wealth, combined with the enterprise of its nine million residents, accounts for an astonishing 20 per cent of sub-Saharan Africa's GDP.

Johannesburg and gold remain all but synonymous – literally so, given that the city's Sotho name Gauteng and Zulu name Egoli both translate as 'Place of Gold'. It is easy to forget, however, that prior to 1886, the craggy Mpumalanga escarpment – which drops from the grassy highveld plateau east of Johannesburg to the hot, scrubby lowveld bordering Mozambique – also hosted a gold rush of significant proportions. It started in 1869 with the discovery of gold near Lydenburg, and gathered further momentum in 1873, when Alec 'Wheelbarrow' Patterson found further alluvial deposits at Pilgrim's Rest. The alluvial gold was all but worked out by the mid-1880s, but underground mining continued until the 1920s. More recently, Pilgrim's Rest was restored as a unique living museum, whose unadorned tin-roofed abodes, set at the base of a misty, green valley, evoke the gold-rush era that – for better or for worse – did so much to shape the subsequent development of South Africa.

Effectively a northerly extension of the Drakensberg, the escarpment running through Mpumalanga – an Ndebele name meaning 'Place of the Rising Sun' – hosts some of the largest tracts of forest left in South Africa. Evocatively named cataracts such as Horseshoe Falls, Lone Creek Falls and Bridal Veil Falls tumble through wooded riverine gorges cut deep into the escarpment, while several viewpoints, most famously Pinnacle Rock and God's Window, offer panoramic views across the hazy dry bush below. The scenic centrepiece of this area is the Blyde River Canyon, a stupendous

OPPOSITE: The Kruger National Park and surrounding private reserves are some of the few remaining strongholds left for the endangered African wild dog.
BELOW: Restored nineteenth-century mining houses at the defunct gold-mining village of Pilgrim's Rest.

cycad-studded 80-metre-deep gorge overlooked by a trio of peaks dubbed the Three Rondavels (due to their similarity to African round huts). The southern terminus of the canyon consists of an extraordinary series of water-eroded cylindrical potholes known as Bourke's Luck.

Just as European settlers set about exploiting South Africa's mineral wealth, so too did they plunder its abundant wildlife, descending from the escarpment in the dry malaria-free winter months to hunt on the eastern lowveld – some for the sport of it, others for meat, hide or horn, others still for elephant-borne 'white gold'. By the mid-1890s, the elephant population of the lowveld had been reduced to just one herd of about 25 animals taking refuge in the Olifants Gorge, its black and white rhino were practically extinct, and the already dwindling grazer herds were dealt a further blow in the form of a deadly rinderpest epidemic. That any wildlife survives there today is largely thanks to two men: President Paul Kruger, who set aside a game-depleted tract of land between the Sabie and Crocodile rivers as the Sabie Game Reserve in 1898, and Major James Douglas-Hamilton, the warden who oversaw the reserve's slow, obstacle-strewn recuperation and later fought for its recognition as a national park.

BELOW: Set on the Mpumalanga escarpment, the viewpoint known as God's Window offers a panoramic view across the lowveld of the Kruger National Park and surrounds.
OPPOSITE: Berlin Falls is one of several scenic waterfalls set on the Mpumalanga escarpment.

ABOVE: A young hyena guards its den in the Sabi Sands Game Reserve, an easterly extension of the Kruger Park that incorporates renowned game lodges such as Mala Mala, Sabi Sabi and Londolozi.

The Sabie Game Reserve was the precursor to the Kruger National Park, which was gazetted in 1926, when its borders were extended northward to the Limpopo River to cover almost 20 000 square kilometres. Today, the Kruger Park ranks as one of the world's truly great game reserves, with 147 mammal species recorded, including substantial populations of lion, leopard, cheetah, wild dog and spotted hyena, some 10 000 elephant, 3 500 white and 350 black rhino (all descended from animals introduced from Hluhluwe-Imfolozi), 25 000 buffalo, 32 000 Burchell's zebra, 2 500 hippo, 5 000 giraffe, and a full 22 antelope species, of which the most common are impala (150 000), blue wildebeest (15 000) and greater kudu (7 000).

The fences that once enclosed the Kruger National Park are gradually being torn down. First to go were all physical barriers between the national park and the various private reserves which run along its western boundary. This was followed in 2002 by the removal of the fenced border with Mozambique's Limpopo National Park. The forthcoming addition of Zimbabwe's Gonarezhou National Park and the two areas of communal land dividing it from the Kruger Park will boost the size of the contiguous Great Limpopo Transfrontier Park to 35 000 square kilometres – as well as marking the end of the first phase in a process that may result in a conservation area extending over 100 000 square kilometres.

ABOVE: The Kruger National Park is famous for its dense populations of predators, such as the handsomely hirsute lion, the largest of all terrestrial carnivores in Africa.

Nocturnal animals

Dusk is a magical time in the African bush, offering welcome release from the still heat of the day. Dusk also marks the 'changing of the guard' in Africa's wild places. It's bedtime for diurnal feeders such as monkeys, most antelope, and the overwhelming majority of birds, and generally signals lower levels of activity for elephant, giraffe and warthogs. But it's also when some of the more elusive and fascinating African creatures leap into action, among them the termite-gulping aardvark, the wide-eyed bushbabies, the quill-rustling porcupine, the kangaroo-like springhare, and the banshee-wailing tree hyrax.

Night is when most of Africa's diverse mammalian predators head out on the prowl – including leopards, of course, but also smaller feline species such as serval, caracal and African wild cat. In addition, the sleek-tailed genets, the pugnacious honey badger, and the ponderous civet are also nocturnal. Only at night will you hear the low booming call of lions rumbling across miles of savanna, the eerie rising whoop of the spotted hyena, or the higher yapping of jackals – often underscored by a 'white noise' of chattering insects and the plink-plonk of frogs.

Some of Africa's most spectacular birds are predominantly nocturnal. A low hooting noise from high in the canopy often reveals the presence of an Eagle Owl, while the eagerly sought Pel's Fishing Owl is most often observed flying in the vicinity of water. There are also the nightjars, most of which are so similar as to render sight identification almost impossible. However this is not true of the spectacular Pennant-winged Nightjar, most often seen at dusk with its preposterously long wing-streamers in tow.

The magic of dusk is equalled by that of the African dawn. Preceded by a joyfully infectious riot of birdsong, the first tentative rays of the sun warm the dry, cool air, and the cast of Africa's nocturnal drama retire for the day – sometimes allowing the human intruder one quick glimpse before they retreat to a den or thicket.

*The White-faced Owl (**ABOVE**) and southern lesser bushbaby (**BELOW**) are both almost exclusively nocturnal foragers. Leopards (**OPPOSITE ABOVE**) are most active after dusk. Hippos (**OPPOSITE BELOW**) emerge from their watery daytime haunts to feed on grass and vegetable matter.*

ABOVE: A married Ndebele woman in traditional costume. The geometric wall paintings in the background are typical of Ndebele villages.

The Ndebele of South Africa have been recognized as a distinct culture since the sixteenth century. In 1823 they broke away from the Zulu king Chaka and fled across the Drakensberg into northeast South Africa. As their numbers increased, they migrated to new areas to settle, repeating the pattern as they needed more and more land. The Ndebele raided as far south as the Orange River, destroying or absorbing surrounding tribes, but in the nineteenth century they became involved in a war with the Boers (Afrikaans-speaking white settlers of South Africa's former Transvaal province), which destroyed their traditional way of life, forcing them to live and work on farms. In 1974, the KwaNdebele 'homeland' was created for them by the South African apartheid government.

Contemporary Ndebele live in kraals and are renowned for their sophisticated sense of geometric design, which is used in many aspects of their lives, ranging from objects of adornment to their distinctively painted houses. Ndebele beadwork is highly developed and elaborate, and worn to signify different life stages.

ABOVE: Traditionally an Ndebele woman wears multiple coloured leg bands after she is married.

LEFT: An Ndebele child wears the brightly coloured beads that also adorn the closely related Zulu people.

Beneath the barrier of spears

KWAZULU-NATAL

Perhaps the most topographically and scenically diverse of the nine provinces that comprise South Africa is KwaZulu-Natal. It has an idyllic subtropical coastline, dense coastal bush protected within some of Africa's oldest game reserves, a well-watered escarpment draped in misty forests and rolling green pastures, and the windswept peaks of the Drakensberg. Paradoxically, this relatively small province, which markets itself as the 'Kingdom of the Zulu', and is unique in its recognition of a traditional monarch, is also the country's most culturally cohesive, with borders approximating those of the nineteenth-century empire founded by the iconic military leader Shaka Zulu.

Shaka is among the most controversial figures in African history, not least because his true identity and the exact circumstances surrounding his emergence are, in the words of Norman Etherington, 'beyond the reach of historians' and thus unusually malleable in the name of polemics. The illegitimate son of a chief, Shaka grew up a social outcast, and allegedly also suffered from impediments ranging from a stutter to a deformed penis. Despite this, he single-handedly masterminded the melding of the formerly disparate clans of present-day KwaZulu-Natal into a unified nation, while simultaneously instigating an era of social turmoil and inter-tribal bloodshed – remembered locally as the Mfeqane or 'Crushing' – the repercussions of which were felt as far away as present-day Tanzania.

OPPOSITE: KwaZulu-Natal, and its game reserves in particular, form a vital stronghold for Africa's endangered rhinos.
BELOW: The idyllically isolated Rocktail Bay on the northern coast of KwaZulu-Natal.

ABOVE: Dancing and singing are integral to many indigenous African societies, and the Zulu are no exception. Male dancers traditionally wear costumes made almost exclusively of animal hide, while the entire outfit of a dancing maiden might be made of beads (BELOW). Before the dancing begins, the musicians heat up the hide on their drums to reduce brittleness (RIGHT).

OPPOSITE: A Zulu woman sits in front of her beehive hut, wearing a traditional hat reserved for married women.

272

The international infamy of the Zulu people dates to January 1879, when King Cetshwayo's spear-wielding army massacred a British military encampment at the sphinx-like Isandlwana Hill – the most humiliating defeat ever suffered by Britain at the hands of an African foe. Later that same year, Britain would avenge itself by razing the royal kraal at Ondoni and forcing Cetshwayo into short-lived hiding and eventual capture. But the outmoded notion of the Zulu as ferocious warriors in loincloths still lingers, not least due to the likes of the 1964 film *Zulu* and the more recent television series *Shaka Zulu*.

BELOW: A Zulu chief addresses some of his people on a riverbank in the Zululand region of northern Kwazulu-Natal.

In truth, contemporary KwaZulu-Natal is not significantly more militaristic than anywhere else in Africa, and when it comes to overt traditionalism, the Zulu scarcely compare to the Maasai, for example, or to the Dogon in the west of the continent. All the same, the day-to-day influence of *inyangas* (traditional healers and herbalists) and *sangomas* (spirit diviners and mediums) – not to mention the role of the Zulu monarchy – does, however, remain stronger than superficial appearances might lead one to expect, especially, but not exclusively, in rural areas.

BELOW: Loggerhead turtle hatchlings head out to sea after almost two months of incubation below the sandy beach near Rocktail Bay.

275

Rhinoceros conservation

Africa's second largest terrestrial mammal, the white rhinoceros is a rather placid grazer whose popular name, derived from the Dutch *weit* (wide), actually refers to the square lips that enable it to crop grass so efficiently. Distributed throughout much of Africa in recent prehistory – skeletal remains and rock art depictions are widespread north of the Sahara – the white rhino has since experienced an ongoing decline in its range. This decline may or may not be directly related to human activity, but has certainly been hastened by it in the past.

By the early twentieth century, two racially discrete relict populations survived. The more vulnerable of these was the southern race, represented by the Imfolozi herd of fewer than 20 individuals, from which practically every last one of the estimated 5 000 white rhinos left on our planet today is descended. The northern population, centred on the Uganda-Congo border, was still reasonably common in the colonial era, since when it has suffered as a result of political instability. Today, mirroring the situation in Zululand a century ago, the future of the northern white rhino rests on the survival of one last remaining breeding herd. This herd is resident in a reserve in the eastern Congo that is currently inaccessible to tourists because of civil war.

In the mid-1970s, there seemed to be no specific reason to fear for the future of the continent's 75 000 black rhinos – a scrubland species that's not noticeably darker than its 'white' cousin, but is considerably less bulky, legendarily temperamental, and boasts a distinctive hooked upper lip designed for browsing on tough vegetation. Then a protracted outbreak of commercial rhino-horn poaching gripped the continent, reducing the total population to fewer than 3 500 individuals by 1990. Thankfully, this trend has been reversed, and the continental population is now thought to approach 5 000 animals. But so long as the rhino's horn of compressed hair retains its high commercial value (as an aphrodisiac in Asia and a dagger handle in Yemen), a heavy cloud hangs over the long-term future of Africa's rhinos.

With its hooked upper lip adapted for browsing from thorny trees, the black rhino (ABOVE) can be distinguished from the more placid and flat-lipped white rhino (OPPOSITE). Both species are now endangered, and in many areas they are protected by armed rangers, such as in this sanctuary in Zimbabwe (BELOW).

The epicentre of Zulu political power is the part of KwaZulu-Natal lying north of the Tugela River. Informally but widely referred to as Zululand, this hot, humid, lush and – despite lying south of the tropic of Capricorn – emphatically tropical-looking region is studded with small game reserves such as Mkhuze, Ndumo and Tembe, whose wilderness character evokes East Africa as much as anywhere else in South Africa. The Zululand reserves harbour Africa's densest rhino population, and they also form the main stronghold for the splendid nyala antelope, the male of which – intermediate in size to the affiliated bushbuck and greater kudu – is distinguished by a shaggy chestnut-black coat and impressive spiralled horns.

Zululand's largest terrestrial wildlife sanctuary is Hluhluwe-Imfolozi, which consists of its two constituent reserves, both gazetted in 1897, as well as a connecting corridor of state land. Jointly managed since 1989, Hluhluwe-Imfolozi is home to all of the so-called Big Five, with rhino being especially common. Indeed, had it not been for the creation of Imfolozi (formerly Umfolozi), the southern race of white rhino would almost certainly be extinct today. Some 1 800 white rhinos now roam the rolling green hills and valleys of Hluhluwe-Imfolozi, alongside about 500 black rhino, and all the white rhinos found elsewhere in southern Africa descend from animals relocated from this one reserve.

Fed by the Hluhluwe, Imfolozi and Mkhuze rivers, the St Lucia Estuary – recently accorded World Heritage Site status by the United Nations Educational, Scientific and Cultural Organization (UNESCO) – extends over an area of 325 square kilometres to form Africa's largest estuarine system. The vast freshwater estuary, which harbours South Africa's densest hippo and crocodile populations, is now protected within a network of small reserves collectively known as the Greater St Lucia Wetland Park. Separated from the estuary by the world's tallest forested dunes, the coastline north of the St Lucia mouth is a pivotal breeding ground for marine turtles, while the ecosystem as a whole supports over 500 bird species, ranging from the aquatic Pink-backed Pelican and Mangrove Kingfisher to the strictly terrestrial Gorgeous Bush-Shrike and Purple-crested Turaco.

A very different type of wilderness runs along KwaZulu-Natal's 200-kilometre border with Lesotho. This is the central Drakensberg, or as the Zulu people who live in its shadow know it, uKhahlamba – 'The Barrier of Spears' – a sequence of craggy blue peaks so formidable that even today just one rocky road links KwaZulu-Natal with Lesotho. The highest part of a 1 000-kilometre-long mountain range that spans four South African provinces as well as the kingdoms of Swaziland and Lesotho, and the one part of the country to receive snow on a near-annual basis, the central Drakensberg is now protected within a patchwork of pedestrian-friendly reserves referred to collectively as the uKhahlamba-Drakensberg Park.

A highlight of uKhahlamba-Drakensberg Park is the magnificently scenic Royal Natal National Park, whose dramatic montane landscapes include an unbroken 8-kilometre-long sandstone escarpment known as the Amphitheatre, the 3 282-metre peak of Mont-aux-Sources (as its name hints, the source of three major river systems), and the 850-metre Tugela Falls. By contrast, the more southerly Giant's Castle Game Reserve is best known for its wildlife – eland are common, while a special vulture hide is the most reliable place in southern Africa for sightings of the stately Lammergeier or Bearded Vulture. The main cave also houses a superb rock art panel, among the finest of 600 similar sites within the uKhahlamba-Drakensberg Park. Collectively the sites contain a total of 35 000 paintings that are attributed to the San (or Bushman) hunter-gatherers who inhabited these mountains until the mid-nineteenth century – making it quite possibly the richest collection of rock art anywhere in the world.

OPPOSITE: Zululand is home to the giraffe, which stands up to six metres high and is the world's tallest terrestrial animal.
ABOVE: The handsome, but shy nyala.
OVERLEAF: The Amphitheatre in the Drakensberg consists of an 8-km-long sandstone 'wall' between a pair of 3000-metre-high rock formations, which are known as the Eastern Buttress and the Sentinel.

279

Rock art

The Drakensberg is one of several parts of Africa – others include the central Zimbabwean Plateau, the Maasai Escarpment in Tanzania, and the Air Mountains of Niger – whose wealth of prehistoric rock art is, in the words of archaeologist Peter Garlake, 'one of the world's last and greatest undiscovered artistic and cultural treasures'.

Exposure to these ancient African artworks prompts three obvious questions: How old are they? Who painted them? What was their intent? The simple answer is that nobody really knows. The rock art of sub-Saharan Africa is often referred to as 'Bushman painting' – a somewhat presumptuous label given that the oldest paintings date back 10 000 years or more. That the artists were hunter-gatherers is implicit in their subject matter, but their relationship to the so-called Bushmen who occupied Africa's dry southwest until they were hunted out by European settlers is anybody's guess.

Two schools of thought surround rock-art interpretation. The first is that the paintings were recreational or documentary in intent, while the second is that they are primarily of ritual significance. Resolving this question is complicated by the likelihood that the extant galleries represent a fraction of a percentage of the art executed at the time. We have no record of whether the artists dabbled on canvases less durable than rock. However, unless one assumes that posterity was a conscious goal, it seems more than probable.

One of the most striking sub-Saharan rock panels is Diana's Vow in Zimbabwe, which is dominated by a metre-long humanoid figure with a sable-like head, a tendril emerging from its enlarged penis, a large spotted oval hump, and one arm raised as if carrying a tray. The first Europeans to see this painting assumed the artist to be from some other region, and it does rather evoke the stylized art of Ancient Egypt. But more likely the figure is an entranced shaman whose spotted torso and hump symbolize his potency, as – rather less subtly – do the ornate genitalia. Ultimately, however, it is perhaps less important that we 'understand' Africa's prehistoric art than that we recognize its significance – the sole testament to an otherwise mute culture more complex than those who exterminated its inheritors could ever have imagined.

ABOVE: About 3 000 years old, this series of rock engravings depicting cattle, near the Ethiopian town of Dilla, forms some of the earliest evidence of pastoralism in sub-Saharan Africa.
BELOW: This panel of surreal human-like figures or 'crocodile men' lies in the rocky suburbs of the Zimbabwean capital of Harare.
OPPOSITE: The rock panel Diana's Vow in Zimbabwe.

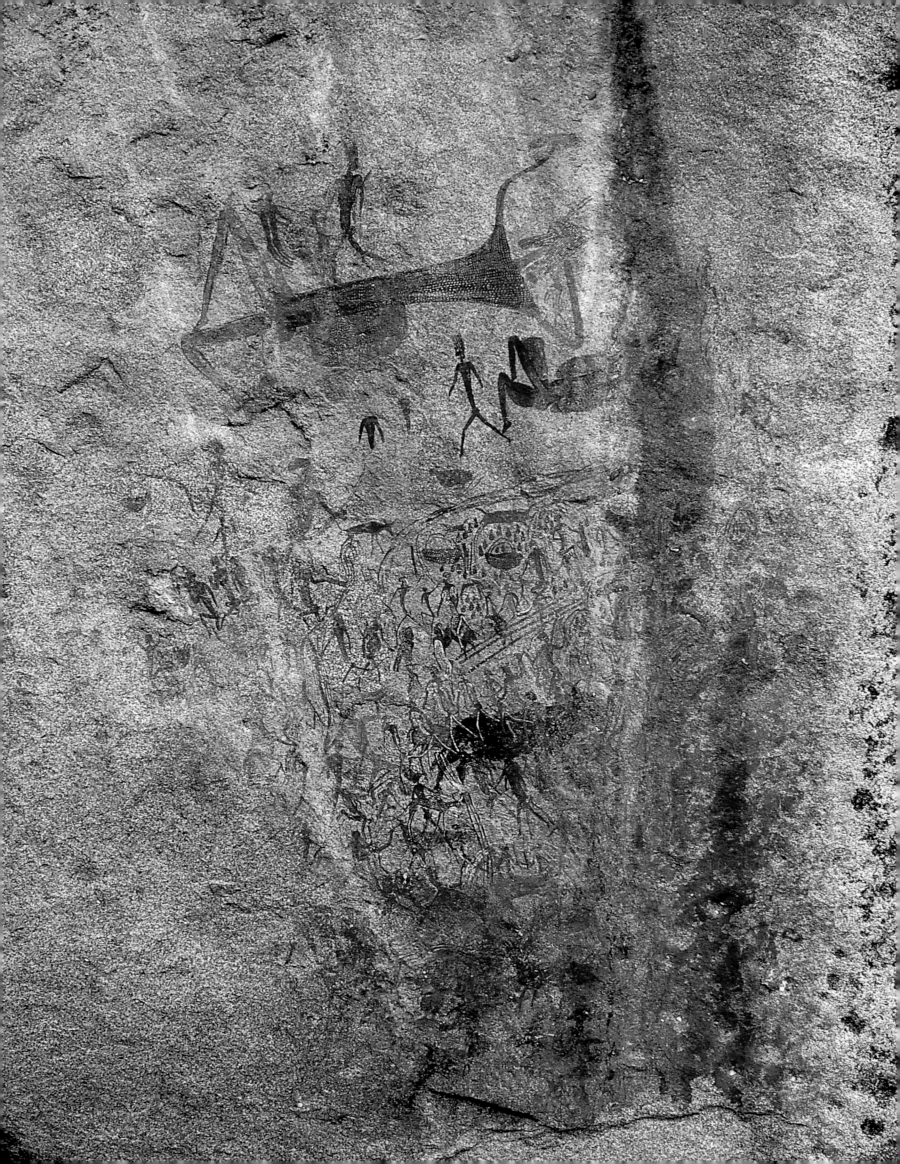

The Fairest Cape

CAPE TOWN AND THE SOUTHERN COASTLINE

In January 1488, Bartolomeu Dias, blown off course by a vicious southeaster, unwittingly attained the milestone that had motivated half a century of Portuguese naval exploration when he rounded the 'Cape of Africa' to enter the Indian Ocean. It was only on the return trip, however, that he obtained the first European view of what he assumed to be the continent's most southerly point: a tall, rocky and potentially treacherous peninsula that he named Cabo Tormentoso – The Cape of Storms.

Today, Dias's tormentor is better known as the Cape of Good Hope, a name bequeathed from afar by the delighted King John of Portugal shortly after his subject's return to Lisbon. And Dias was mistaken in thinking that it formed the southern tip of Africa, a distinction that falls instead on the altogether more bleak-looking Cape Agulhas, whose needle-sharp offshore rocks have wrecked more that 200 ships over the centuries. But his error is understandable: the majestic cliffs that guard the southern tip of the 50-kilometre-long Cape Peninsula, lapped by the Indian Ocean to the east and the Atlantic to the west, genuinely do possess a presence befitting the end – or, if you prefer, the beginning – of a continent.

Historically, the Cape Peninsula is the pivot linking the end of one world to the beginning of another. In 1580, when Sir Francis Drake proclaimed it to be 'the most stately thing and the fairest Cape we saw in the whole circumference of the earth', the peninsula was still occupied by the Khoisan-speaking sheep-herders and hunter-gatherers who had prevailed in the region for millennia. Then, in 1652, Jan van Riebeeck established South Africa's first permanent European settlement – the future Cape Town – at the northern end of the Cape Peninsula, below the distinctive silhouette of Table Mountain. Within 200 years, the Khoisan-speakers had vanished – some victim to exotic diseases, others killed or driven northward by gun-toting settlers, others still integrated into the mixed-race community known today as Cape coloureds.

OPPOSITE: The exclusive Cape Town suburb of Llandudno has a sparkling setting at the western base of the rocky cliffs that characterize the Cape Peninsula.
BELOW: A sweet vendor relaxes at his stall in the township of Khayelitsha on the Cape Flats near Cape Town.

Namaqualand

First impressions can be deceptive. The Karoo – the vast tract of stony semi-desert that covers much of the western half of South Africa – is a classic case in point. Flat, dry and somewhat featureless, the Karoo typically receives just 150 millimetres of rainfall annually, and superficially it seems bereft of life. Yet this remarkable semi-desert, whose name derives from a Khoisan word meaning 'Place of Thirst', is listed alongside Tanzania's Eastern Arc Mountains and the forested Albertine Rift as one of the world's top 25 biodiversity hotspots, thanks to a remarkable floral diversity that includes some 600 endemic species listed as rare or endangered in the World Conservation Union (IUCN) Red Book.

Something like 1 700 succulent species – more than 10 per cent of the global total – occur in the Karoo, most of them endemic. True, for much of the year this diversity of hardy plants is less than apparent to the untrained eye. But not so in August and September, when the region receives its meagre annual rainfall, and its 400 species of spring annuals erupt in colourful wild flower displays that attract botanical enthusiasts from all around the world.

The epicentre of the wild flower displays is the northerly part of the Karoo known as Namaqualand, where the harsh and sparsely populated landscape of rocky plains and craggy mountains is suddenly transformed into a multi-hued carpet of daisies – orange, yellow, pink, white and purple – as well as mesembryanthemums, violets, gladioli and numerous other genera. It's a wonderful spectacle, the botanical equivalent of the Serengeti migration or the flamingos that flock on East Africa's Rift Valley lakes. And it is no less remarkable when one realizes that this floral diversity is a modern phenomenon – it is thought that most of the area's plant species evolved within the past 10 000 to 15 000 years as a result of climatic change.

ABOVE: Daisy-like Tripteris oppositifolia bloom in colourful abundance amid a stand of somewhat less floral kokerbooms (quiver trees) (OPPOSITE).
BELOW: Colourful wild flower displays abound in spring.

The Cape Peninsula is something of an ecological island, thanks to its so-called Mediterranean climate, which, unlike the rest of southern Africa, is characterized by dry summers and rainy winters. Its borders define the Cape Floristic Region – the smallest of the world's six recognized floral kingdoms. It extends over a mere 90 000 square kilometres, yet is home to over 8 500 flowering plant species, of which two-thirds occur nowhere else in the world. As some measure of this region's extraordinary floral diversity, a greater number of indigenous plant species have been identified in the small nature reserve at the Cape of Good Hope, than in the whole of the British Isles.

The region's predominant vegetation is a low, heath-like ground cover known as fynbos (fine bush), which can appear rather drab at first glance, but on closer inspection reveals a rich sprinkling of subtle pastel hues that explode into flamboyant colour during the spring wild flower season. A feature of the region is its diversity of regal proteas, most of which flower in the winter. High levels of endemism are noted among the region's invertebrates and cold-blooded vertebrates, and eight bird species are more-or-less unique to fynbos habitats, including the emblematic Cape Sugarbird, whose long curved bill is designed to drink protea nectar.

BELOW: No less iconic and even more ancient than the pyramids that cap the opposite end of the continent, Table Mountain looms over Cape Town and Table Bay near the southernmost tip of Africa.

The Cape's climatic similarities to the Mediterranean led Van Riebeeck to dabble in viniculture within three years of his arrival, albeit with mixed success. The arrival of the first Huguenot settlers in 1687 led to a rapid improvement in standards, so that within two decades the sweet wines made at Constantia were of sufficient merit to export to the courts of Europe. Today, more than 100 000 hectares of the Cape are given over to vineyards, and South Africa ranks as the world's fifth-largest wine producer. Constantia, nestled on the eastern slopes of Table Mountain, remains an active producer, but the main centre of viniculture is the mountainous country surrounding the towns of Stellenbosch and Franschhoek, which also host some of the finest examples of the region's distinctive Cape Dutch architecture.

Dias's crew became the first Europeans to set foot on South African soil when they landed at Mossel Bay, which is divided from Cape Town by some 400 kilometres of coastline. Today this coastal stretch is known for offering some of the world's most reliable land-based whale watching during the breeding season, which lasts from August to October. Mossel Bay also marks the beginning of the Garden Route, a ruggedly scenic 200-kilometre stretch of coastline that blends fynbos vegetation with lush evergreen forest, wide sandy beaches, expansive blue lagoons and tall jagged cliffs, such as those that enclose the spectacular Storms River Mouth in the Tsitsikamma National Park.

While whales and dolphins remain common offshore, the Cape's large land-dwelling mammals have been ill served by three centuries of European settlement. The quagga, a zebra-like equid with an unstriped rump, was hunted to extinction in the nineteenth

PREVIOUS PAGE: The extensive winelands and the mountainous hinterland of the Cape Peninsula are dotted with some fine examples of Cape Dutch architecture, such as this homestead at the Dornier Estate near Stellenbosch.

century. The only remaining bluebuck – velvet-coated relatives of the sable and roan antelopes – are four faded specimens housed in a museum. Gone, too, are the hirsute lions that formerly prowled the Cape Peninsula, the hippos that gave their name to Zeekoeivlei on the Cape Flats, and pretty much any other four-legged creature larger than a sheep. Other species have been more fortunate, but only slightly so: the fynbos-associated bontebok was rescued from global extinction by the efforts of one family that set aside part of their farm as a sanctuary for the last 27 semi-domestic individuals, while the few hundred surviving Cape mountain zebra are all descended from a 1950 bottle-neck population of just seven females.

The Cape's once plentiful elephants have undergone a similar last-gasp rescue mission. Just 11 individuals survived in 1931, when a tract of dense bush to the north of Port Elizabeth was set aside to form the Addo Elephant National Park. By 1968, the number of elephants in Addo had increased to 50, and 10 years later it topped the century mark. Today, more than 400 pachyderms roam the park, their gene pool recently boosted by the relocation of eight bulls from the Kruger National Park. Addo is also home to the Cape's last wild populations of rhino, buffalo and lion – the lions having been reintroduced from the Kalahari in 2003. In the most holistic conservation effort yet associated with the Cape, the core 200-square-kilometre national park has, since 1997, been extended northward to the Karoo and southward to the coast to form the 12 500-square-kilometre Greater Addo National Park, which protects five of South Africa's seven terrestrial biomes, and has the capacity to support at least 2 000 elephants.

BELOW: Dolphins can often be seen frolicking off the Cape coast.

TOP: The west coast of South Africa supports some impressive breeding colonies of marine birds, such as Hartlaub's Gull. LEFT AND ABOVE: The rather comic Jackass or African Penguin is most easily observed en masse at Boulders Beach, just south of Cape Town.

Bird Island at Lambert's Bay hosts innumerable breeding pairs of Cape Cormorants (RIGHT) and Cape Gannets (BELOW).

BIBLIOGRAPHY

The text in this book is the condensed product of 15 years' travelling in, reading about, and writing about Africa. As such, certain sections draw heavily on my own more extensive writings on the same subject, notably my travel guides to South Africa, Mozambique, Malawi, Tanzania, Uganda, Ethiopia, Rwanda, Ghana and East and southern Africa, published by Bradt Travel Guides, and several articles that first appeared in *Africa Geographic* or *Travel Africa*. And while it would be impossible to list every printed and online source for this text – in essence, every book or website I have read about Africa in the past two decades – the following titles were all referred to during the course of researching and writing this book.

Agnese, G. and Re, M. 2003. *Ancient Egypt: Art and Archaeology*. American University in Cairo Press: Cairo.

Ajayi, F. and Espie, E. (eds) 1965. *A Thousand Years of West African History*. Thomas Nelson: Nairobi.

Anquandah, K.J. 1999. *Castles & Forts of Ghana* Ghana Museums & Monuments Board: Accra.

Bradt, H. 2004. *Madagascar: The Bradt Travel Guide*. Seventh edition. Bradt: Chalfont St Peter.

Brown, M. 1989. *Where Giants Trod*. Quiller Press: London.

Brush, E. (ed.). 1982. *Masked Dancers of West Africa: The Dogon*. Time-Life Books: Amsterdam.

Buah, F. 1974. *West Africa Since AD 1000*. Macmillan: London.

Bulpin, T.V. 1980. *Discovering Southern Africa*. TV Bulpin Publications: Cape Town.

Davidson, B. 1977. *A History of West Africa 1000–1800*. Longman: London.

Debrah, I.N. (ed.) 1999. *Asante Traditional Buildings*. Ghana Museums & Monuments Board: Accra.

De Vere, A.J. 1992. *Swahili Origins*. James Currey: London.

Farfour, G., Fletcher, J., Humphreys, A., Jenkins, S., and Sattin, A. 2004. *Egypt*. Seventh edition. Lonely Planet: Footscray.

Giday, B. 1988. *Ethiopian Civilisation*. Belai Giday: Addis Ababa.

Hall, R. 1996. *Empires of the Monsoon: A History of the Indian Ocean and its Invaders*. Harper Collins: London.

Henze, P. 2000. *Layers of Time: A History of Ethiopia*. Hurst: London.

Kingdon, J. 1990. *Island Africa*. Collins: London.

Kingdon, J. 1997. *Field Guide to African Mammals*. Academic Press: San Diego.

Kyeremateng, K. 1996. *The Akans of Ghana*. Sebewie Publishers: Accra.

Last, J. 1982. *Endemic Mammals of Ethiopia*. Ethiopian Tourist Commission: Addis Ababa.

McGuinness, J. 2002. *Morocco Handbook*. Third edition. Footprint: London.

McIntyre, C. 1998. *Namibia: The Bradt Travel Guide*. Bradt: Chalfont St Peter.

McIntyre, C. 2003. *Botswana: The Bradt Travel Guide*. Bradt: Chalfont St Peter.

Moorehead, A. 1960. *The White Nile*. Hamish Hamilton: London.

Moorehead, A. 1962. *The Blue Nile*. Hamish Hamilton: London.

Morris, P. and Jacobs, D. 2001. *Rough Guide to Tunisia*. Sixth edition. Rough Guides: London.

Munro-Hay, S. 1991. *Aksum: An African Civilisation of Late Antiquity*. Edinburgh University Press: Edinburgh.

Nziga, R. 1997. *Peoples & Cultures of Uganda*. Fountain: Kampala.

Oakes, D. (ed.) 1988. *Illustrated History of South Africa*. Reader's Digest: Cape Town.

Obeng, E. 1984. *Ancient Ashanti Chieftaincy*. Ghana Publishing Corporation: Accra.

Onwubiko, K. 1982. *History of West Africa 1000–1800* Africana FEP: Lagos.

Onwubiko, K. 1985. *History of West Africa 1800–Present Day*. Africana FEP: Lagos.

Pakenham, T. 1991. *The Scramble for Africa*. Weidenfield & Nicolson: London.

Portman, I. 1989. *Luxor*. American University in Cairo: Cairo.

Richardson, D. 2003. *Rough Guide to Egypt*. Fifth edition. Rough Guide: London.

Rogerson, B. 1998. *A Travellers' History of North Africa*. Windrush Press: Moreton-in-Marsh.

Shaw, I. and Nicholson, P. 1995. *British Museum Dictionary of Ancient Egypt*. American University in Cairo: Cairo.

Siliotti, A. 2000. *Islamic Cairo* American University in Cairo: Cairo.

Siliotti, A. 2003. *Illustrated Guide to the Pyramids*. American University in Cairo: Cairo.

Sillero-Zuburi, C., and Macdonald, D. 1997. *The Simien Wolf: Status Survey & Conservation Action Plan*. IUCN: Cambridge.

Stuart, C. and Stuart, T. 1997. *Field Guide to the Larger Mammals of Africa*. Struik: Cape Town.

Taylor, S. 1995. *Shaka's Children*. Harper Collins: London.

Van Dantzig, A. 1980. *Forts and Castles of Ghana*. Sedco: Addis Ababa.

Velton, R. 2000. *Mali: The Bradt Travel Guide*. Bradt: Chalfont St Peter.

Willett, D. 2001. *Tunisia*. Second edition. Lonely Planet: Footscray.

PHOTOGRAPHIC CREDITS

ARIADNE VAN ZANDBERGEN 1-3, 6-9, 19 (centre & bottom), 20-41, 46-48, 52-53 (top), 54-57, 59 (top), 60-61, 64-65, 71 (centre & bottom right), 72-97, 99 (top right), 102-115, 131-137, 142, 147, 151, 154-164, 170-181, 192-193, 194-201, 206-211, 215, 218-219, 223-225, 229-231, 234-237, 240-243, 256-265, 271, 272 (bottom right), 273-274, 278-285, 288-291, 295 (top), back cover

MARTIN HARVEY front cover, 4-5, 10, 12-19 (left and top), 42-45, 49-51, 53 (bottom), 58, 59 (bottom), 62-63, 66-71 (top right), 98-99 (top left, left and bottom), 100-101, 116-130, 138-141, 143-146, 148-150, 152-153, 165-169, 182-191, 194, 202-205, 212-213, 216-217, 220-222, 226-228, 232-233, 238-239, 244-255, 266-270, 272 (top and bottom left), 275-277, 286-287, 294, 295-296 (bottom)

GERHARD DREYER / IMAGES OF AFRICA 286 (bottom)

THOMAS P. PESCHAK 292-293